Bond
No.1 for exam success

Maths

Assessment Papers

8-9 years

OXFORD
UNIVERSITY PRESS

OXFORD
UNIVERSITY PRESS

Great Clarendon Street, Oxford, OX2 6DP, United Kingdom

Oxford University Press is a department of the University of Oxford.
It furthers the University's objective of excellence in research, scholarship,
and education by publishing worldwide. Oxford is a registered trade mark of
Oxford University Press in the UK and in certain other countries

Text © J M Bond and Andrew Baines 2015
Illustrations © Oxford University Press 2015

The moral rights of the authors have been asserted

First published in 2015
This edition published in 2021

All rights reserved. No part of this publication may be reproduced,
stored in a retrieval system, or transmitted, in any form or by any
means, without the prior permission in writing of Oxford University
Press, or as expressly permitted by law, by licence or under terms
agreed with the appropriate reprographics rights organization.
Enquiries concerning reproduction outside the scope of the above
should be sent to the Rights Department, Oxford University Press, at
the address above.

You must not circulate this work in any other form and you must
impose this same condition on any acquirer

British Library Cataloguing in Publication Data
Data available

978-0-19-277994-6

10 9 8 7 6 5 4 3 2 1

Paper used in the production of this book is a natural, recyclable
product made from wood grown in sustainable forests.
The manufacturing process conforms to the environmental
regulations of the country of origin.

Printed in China

Acknowledgements

The publishers would like to thank the following for permissions to
use copyright material:

Page make-up: OKS Prepress, India
Illustrations: Tech-Set Limited
Cover illustrations: Lo Cole

Although we have made every effort to trace and contact all
copyright holders before publication this has not been possible in all
cases. If notified, the publisher will rectify any errors or omissions at
the earliest opportunity.

Links to third party websites are provided by Oxford in good faith
and for information only. Oxford disclaims any responsibility for
the materials contained in any third party website referenced in
this work.

Before you get started

What is Bond?

This book is part of the Bond Assessment Papers series for maths, which provides **thorough and continuous practice of all the key maths content** from ages five to thirteen. Bond's maths resources are ideal preparation for many different kinds of tests and exams – from SATs to 11+ and other secondary school selection exams.

What does this book cover?

It covers all the maths that a child of this age would be expected to learn and is fully in line with the National Curriculum for maths and the National Numeracy Strategy. One of the key features of Bond Assessment Papers is that each one practises **a wide variety of skills and question types** so that children are always challenged to think – and don't get bored repeating the same question type again and again. We think that variety is the key to effective learning. It helps children 'think on their feet' and cope with the unexpected.

The age given on the cover is for guidance only. As the papers are designed to be reasonably challenging for the age group, any one child may naturally find him or herself working above or below the stated age. The important thing is that children are always encouraged by their performance. Working at the right level is the key to this.

What does the book contain?

- **24 papers** – each one contains 40 questions.
- **Scoring devices** – there are score boxes in the margins and a Progress Chart on page 64. The chart is a visual and motivating way for children to see how they are doing. Encouraging them to colour in the chart as they go along and to try to beat their last score can be highly effective!
- **Next Steps** – advice on what to do after finishing the papers can be found on the inside back cover.
- **Answers** – located in an easily-removed central pull-out section.
- **Key maths words** – on page 1 you will find a glossary of special key words that are used in the papers. These are highlighted in bold each time that they appear. These words are now used in the maths curriculum and children are expected to know them at this age.

How can you use this book?

One of the great strengths of Bond Assessment Papers is their flexibility. They can be used at home, school and by tutors to:

- provide regular maths practice in **bite-sized chunks**
- **highlight strengths and weaknesses** in the core skills

- identify **individual needs**
- set **homework**
- set **timed formal practice** tests – allow about 30 minutes.

It is best to start at the beginning and work though the papers in order.

What does a score mean and how can it be improved?

If children colour in the Progress Chart at the back, this will give you an idea of how they are doing. The Next Steps inside the back cover will help you to decide what to do next to help a child progress. We suggest that it is always valuable to go over any wrong answers with children.

Don't forget the website …!

Visit www.bond11plus.co.uk for lots of advice, information and suggestions on everything to do with Bond, exams, and helping children to do their best.

Key words

Some special maths words are used in this book. You will find them in **bold** each time they appear in the papers. These words are explained here.

area	the space inside a shape. Area is measured in square units, for example square centimetres (cm^2) or square metres (m^2)
cube	a solid shape whose faces are all squares, such as a child's building block
cuboid	a solid shape whose faces are either all rectangles, or rectangles and squares such as a cereal packet
digit	any single number, for example 4 has one digit, 37 has two digits, 437 has three digits
divisible	can be divided by, for example 4 is divisible by 2
equilateral triangle	a triangle which has all its sides of the same length
faces	flat sides of a solid object
heptagon	a shape with seven sides
hexagon	a shape with six sides
isosceles triangle	a triangle which has two sides the same length
mirror line	the line in which a shape can be reflected, like the reflection in a mirror
multiple	a number which another number multiplies into, for example 3, 6, 9, 12, 15, 60, 93 are multiples of 3
net	the flat shape that a three-dimensional object, such as a box, will make if you open it out
octagon	a shape with 8 sides
parallelogram	a four-sided shape that has its opposite sides parallel
pentagon	a shape with five sides
perimeter	the distance round the outside of a shape
pictogram	a diagram that records something using pictures
polygon	a shape with three or more sides
product	the answer when you multiply two numbers together, for example the product of 4 and 2 is 8
quadrilateral	a shape with 4 sides
round	means roughly or approximately, for example 42 rounded to the nearest 10 is 40, 470 rounded to the nearest 100 is 500
semicircle	a shape which is half a circle
square	a square is a rectangle with four equal sides
sum	the answer when you add two numbers together. The sum of 2 and 4 is 6
symmetry	if a shape has symmetry it has one or more mirror lines like this:
tetrahedron	a solid shape with four triangular faces
Venn diagram	a chart for sorting information of different kinds

Paper 1

The area of this square ☐ = 1, what is the area of each of the shapes below?

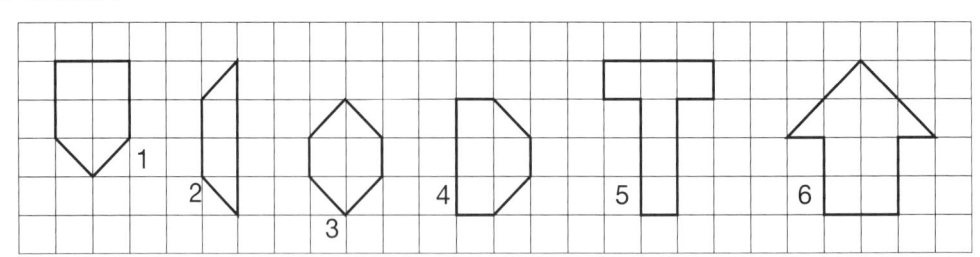

1 _____   2 _____

3 _____   4 _____

5 _____   6 _____

7 Rachel is twice as old as Amy. If Amy is 7, how old is Rachel? _14_

8 How many faces does this **cube** have? _6_

9 Underline the correct answer. Each face on the **cube** is:

   a triangle   <u>a square</u>   a circle   a rectangle

10 How many **faces** does this **cuboid** have? _6_

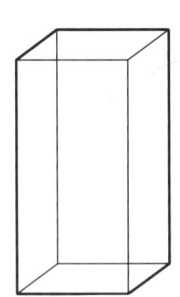

11 Underline the correct answer. Each face on the **cuboid** is:

   a triangle   a square   a circle   <u>a rectangle</u>

There are 60 minutes in an hour. How many minutes are there between:

12 06:19 and 06:30 _____

13 02:27 and 02:50 _____

14 05:50 and 06:10 _____

15 07:51 and 08:00 _____

16 12:01 and 12:40 _____

17 04:52 and 05:10 _____

Underline the correct answer on each line.

18 100 − 29 =   81   79   71   89   129
19 56 ÷ 7 =   8   9   7   6   10
20 47 + 35 =   72   73   81   71   82
21 $\frac{1}{2} + \frac{1}{2} =$ $\frac{1}{4}$ $\frac{1}{2}$ 1   2   4

22–23 Fill in the missing numbers on this number line.

−2   −1   ____   1   ____   3   4

24–25 Fill in the missing numbers on this number line.

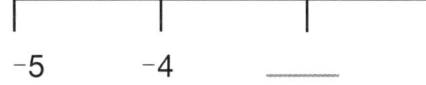

−5   −4   ____   −2   ____   0   1

26–29 Fill in the missing numbers on this number line.

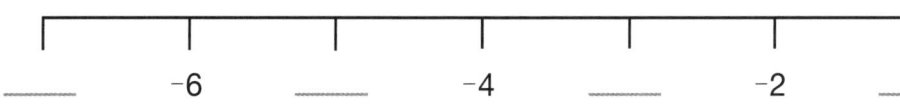

____   −6   ____   −4   ____   −2   ____

Maria was born 5 July 2004.   Anita was born 19 April 2004.
Daley was born 31 October 2004.   David was born 8 June 2003.

30–31 _____ is the eldest and _____ is the youngest.

32–34 On 5 July 2006 Maria was _____ , Anita was _____ and _____ was 3.

35–37 ×6

12	
20	
40	

38–40 +5

60	
80	
90	

Now go to the Progress Chart to record your score!   Total   40

Paper 2

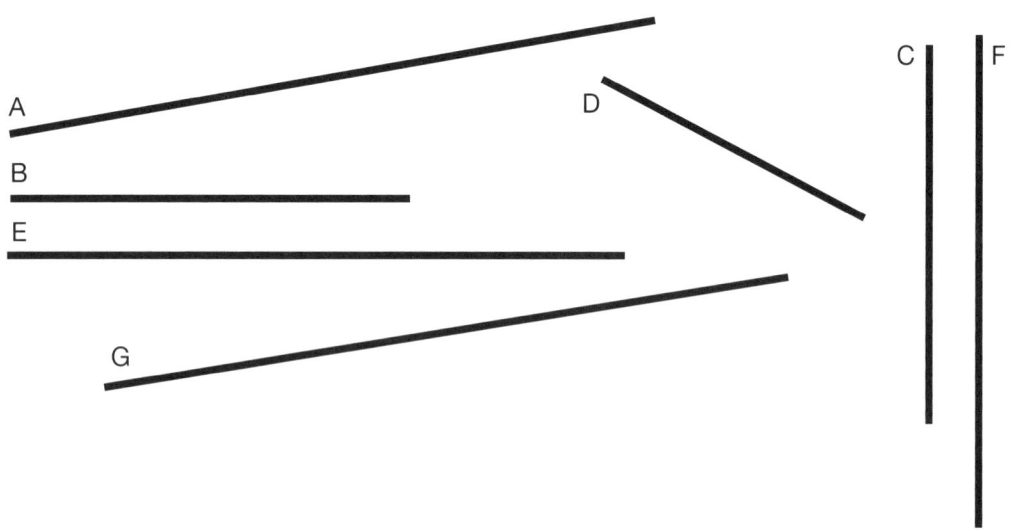

Measure each line and answer the questions.

1 The longest sloping line is _____ .

2 The longest vertical line is _____ .

3 The longest horizontal line is _____ .

4 What is the difference in length between the two horizontal lines? _____ cm

5 What is the difference in length between the two vertical lines? _____ cm

6 The two vertical lines added together are _____ cm long.

7 The two horizontal lines added together are _____ cm long.

8 What is the **product** of 5 and 7?

There are 60 children altogether in Class 2 and Class 3.

9 If there are 32 in Class 2, how many are in Class 3?

George has three times as much money as Michael.

10 Michael has 14p, so how much has George?

312   123   321

11 In which number is the figure 1 a unit?

12 In which number is the figure 1 a ten?

13 In which number is the figure 1 a hundred?

14 What number needs to go in the box? Write it in.

4732 = ☐ + 700 + 30 + 2

15 What number needs to go in the box? Write it in.

5935 = 5000 + ☐ + 30 + 5

16 What number needs to go in the box? Write it in.

3941 = 3000 + 900 + ☐ + 1

17 What number needs to go in the box? Write it in.

5864 = 5000 + 800 + 60 + ☐

18 What number needs to go in the box? Write it in.

9573 = ☐ + 500 + 70 + 3

19 What number needs to go in the box? Write it in.

1633 = 1000 + ☐ + 30 + 3

20 What number needs to go in the box? Write it in.

7488 = 7000 + 400 + ☐ + 8

21–22 Fill in the missing numbers on this number line.

13   15   17   19   ___   23   25   ___

Underline the correct answer in each line.

23	£1 – 11p	=	1p	89p	£1.11	99p	£1.01
24	8p + 6p + 7p	=	20p	22p	19p	21p	23p
25	66 + 26	=	92	87	82	83	93
26	105 ÷ 3	=	15	33	35	41	51
27	$\frac{1}{2}$ of 40	=	80	10	2	40	20
28	1000 ÷ 10	=	500	10	20	100	1000

Mum, Dad, Helen and Andrew went to the zoo.

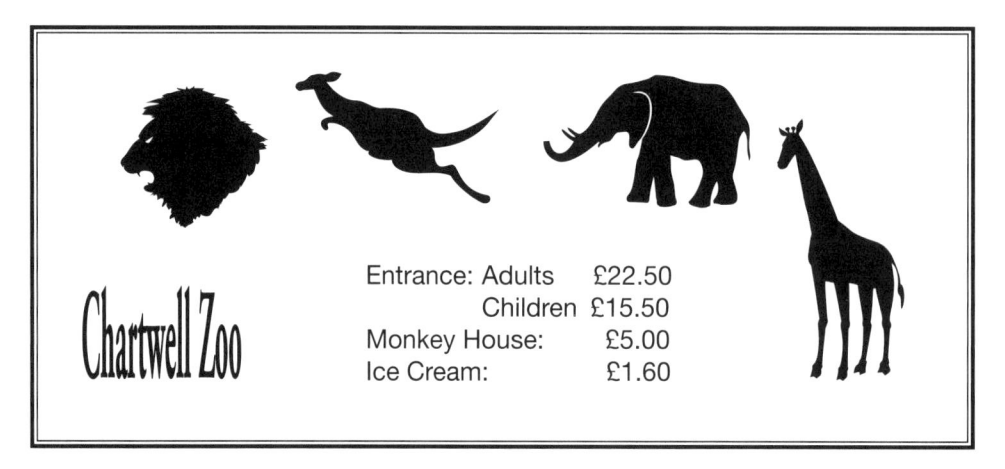

Chartwell Zoo

Entrance: Adults £22.50
Children £15.50
Monkey House: £5.00
Ice Cream: £1.60

29 How much did it cost for all of them to go in? _____

30 How much did it cost for all of them to go in the monkey house? _____

31 How much did it cost for all of them to have an ice cream? _____

32 How much did they spend at the zoo altogether? _____

There were 35 children in a class.

33–34 If the number of boys was one more than the number of girls, there are ___ boys and ___ girls.

Here is part of a ruler.

35 How far is it from A to G? _____

36 How far is it from B to E? _____

37 How far is it from D to H? _____

38 How far is it from C to F? _____   4

39 What number, when divided by 9 gives an answer of 6? _____

40 How many times will 10 go into 200? _____   2

Now go to the Progress Chart to record your score!   Total   40

Paper 3

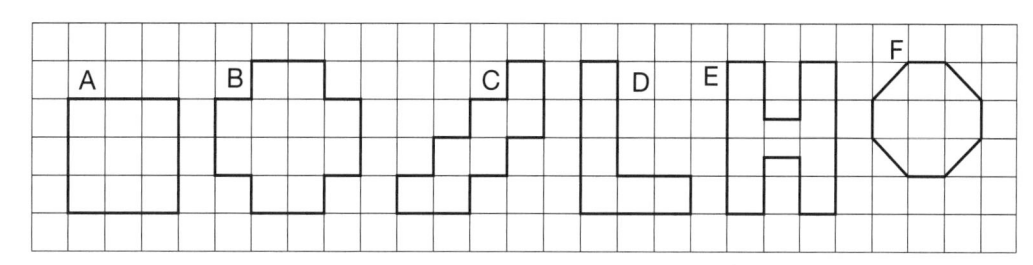

1 The area of shape A is _____ squares.

2 The area of shape B is _____ squares.

3 The area of shape C is _____ squares.

4 The area of shape D is _____ squares.

5 The area of shape E is _____ squares.

6 The area of shape F is _____ squares.   6

7 In every 2 weeks I spend 10 days at school. So in every 5 weeks I spend _____ days at school.

8 In every 3 days I spend 4 hours reading. So in every _____ days I spend 20 hours reading.

9 With every box of cereal you get 4 tokens, and the toy you want requires 24 tokens.
How many boxes of cereal do you have to buy? _____

10 In every *Kid's App* magazine you get 3 transfers. In 3 *Kid's App* magazines you get _____ transfers.

11–15 Underline the numbers which can be divided exactly by 5.

52   25   40   24   45   54   60   51   15

16 Write in words 7001. _____

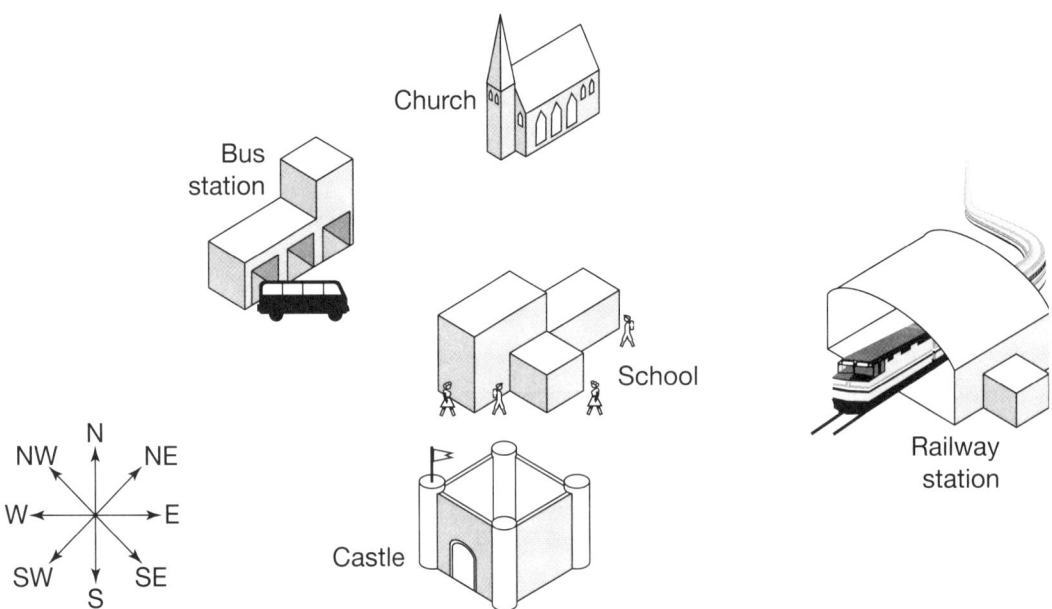

In which direction is:

17 the school from the railway station? _____

18 the castle from the school? _____

19 the bus station from the school? _____

20 the church from the bus station? _____

21 the railway station from church? _____

22 the castle from the church? _____

23 the school from the bus station? _____

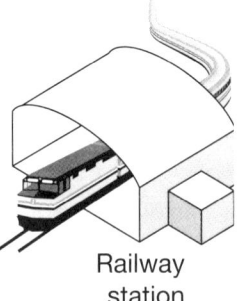

What number is halfway between:

24 50 and 70? _____

25 35 and 55? _____

26 25 and 35? _____

27 12 and 20? _____

28 Jane was born in 2008. Jock is 3 years older than Jane. In what year was he born? _____

29 Leanne was born in 2005. In what year was she 6? _____

30 Rehman was 12 in 2011. In what year was she born? _____

31–33 Reflect these shapes in the **mirror line**.

34 What is the biggest number you can make with these **digits**: 3, 6, 4, 8? _____

35 Now write it in words. _____

36 What is the biggest number you can make with these **digits**: 2, 3, 4, 0? _____

37 Now write it in words. _____

38 Write in figures three thousand, two hundred and fifty-four. _____

39 What is one quarter of 60? _____

40 How many minutes are there between 10:45 and 11:10? _____

Now go to the Progress Chart to record your score!   Total

Paper 4

1. 73
    35
    + 98
    ___

2. 58
    × 6
    ___

3. £6.98
    + £0.42
    ___

4–9 Fill in the missing numbers to balance the scales.

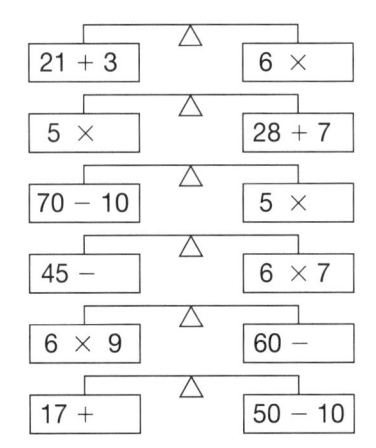

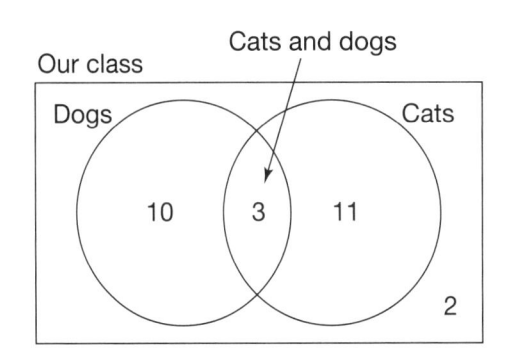

21 + 3	△	6 × ☐
5 × ☐	△	28 + 7
70 − 10	△	5 × ☐
45 − ☐	△	6 × 7
6 × 9	△	60 − ☐
17 + ☐	△	50 − 10

Our class made this **Venn diagram** to show how many of us have cats and dogs.

Our class — Dogs: 10, Cats and dogs: 3, Cats: 11, (outside): 2

10 How many children have dogs?

11 How many have cats?

12 How many have both a cat and a dog?

13 How many children haven't got a dog?

14 How many children haven't got a cat?

15 How many children are there in the class?

16 When a number was added to 16 the answer was 25. What was the number? _____

17 What temperature does this thermometer show? _____

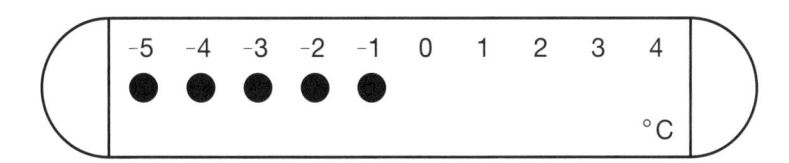

18 Draw a circle around the lowest temperature: −7 °C,   −9 °C

19 Kay was 9 in 2010. In what year was she born? _____

20 Martin was born in December 2007 and Michael was born in January 2008.

   Who is the elder? _____

This **pictogram** shows the number of children in our school.

Key

☺ = 10 children

♀ = 5 children

21 How many children are there in the school? _____

22 In which road or street do most children live? _____

23 Twice as many children live in the High Street as in _____

24 There are three times as many children in Birch Avenue as in _____ .

25–28 Twenty more children come to our school. Five live in Farm Lane, 5 in Riverside Road and 10 in Birch Avenue. Show this on the **pictogram**.

29 How many will there now be in our school? _____

30 How much greater is 33 than 19?

31 I spent 77p and had 15p left. How much did I have at first?

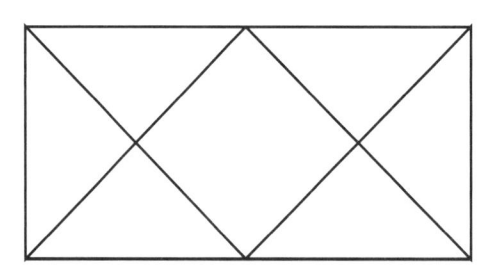

32 What is the cost of 3 packets of crisps at 26p each?

Look closely at the shape above.

33 How many **squares** does it contain?

34 How many rectangles does it contain?

35 How many triangles does it contain?

One question on each line has a different answer from the others.

Draw a line under it.

36	5 × 10	45 + 5	10 × 5	60 – 5	47 + 3
37	7 × 6	4 × 12	6 × 8	42 + 6	50 – 2

38 What number is 1 less than 300?

39 The number which is 2 more than 278 is

40 If I took 10 from 106 it would leave

Now go to the Progress Chart to record your score!   Total   40

Paper 5

1 Draw a circle around the highest temperature: −8 °C,   −9 °C

2–3 Fill in the missing numbers on this number line.

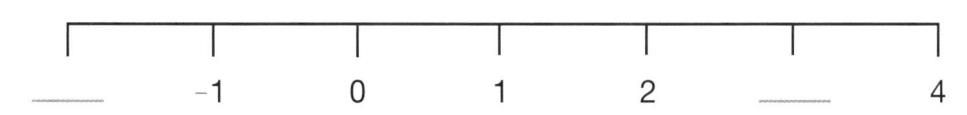

____   −1   0   1   2   ____   4

Underline the correct answer in each line.

4 11 × 11   =   110   111   121   132   122
5 150 ÷ 30 =   50   5   30   20   55
6 70 − 39   =   41   49   39   109   31
7 1½ hours =   75 min 90 min 45 min 85 min 15 min
8 1.5 kg   =   150 g   505 g   1500 g 1050 g 105 g
9 510 ÷ 5   =   21   102   120   12   121
10 150 cm   =   15 m   0.15 m 150 m   50 m   1.5 m

A — 7 cm × 3 cm

11 What is the **area** of rectangle A? _____ cm²
12 What is the **perimeter** of rectangle A? _____ cm

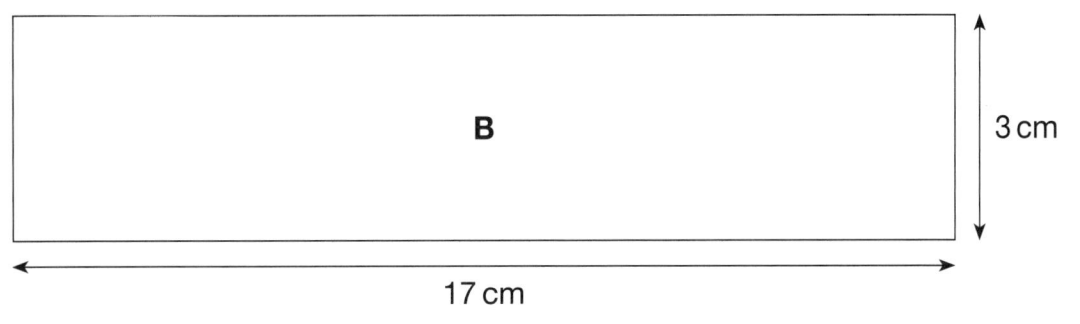

B — 17 cm × 3 cm

13 What is the **area** of rectangle B? _____ cm²
14 What is the **perimeter** of rectangle B? _____ cm

Fill in the missing number in each question.

15 3 + 4 + _____ = 10
16 5 + 1 − _____ = 4
17 3 + 3 + _____ = 9

18–22 Underline the numbers which are **divisible** by 7.

19   49   28   56   62   35   77   79

23–26 Underline the numbers which are **multiples** of 6.

36   72   26   96   56   24   28

Here is part of a centimetre ruler.

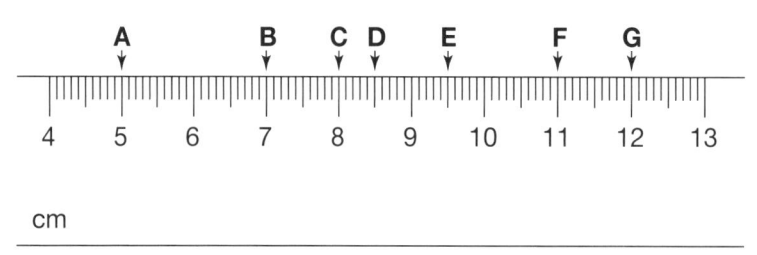

cm

27 How far is it from A to B? _____

28 How far is it from C to D? _____

29 How far is it from A to D? _____

30 How far is it from B to F? _____

31 How far is it from C to G? _____

32 How far is it from E to G? _____

Write the next two numbers in each line.

33–34   6   12   18   24   30   ____ ____

35–36   50   47   44   41   38   ____ ____

Underline the larger of each pair.

37 (6 × 10)   or   (3 × 22)

38 (5 × 20)   or   (11 × 10)

39 (10 × 10) or   (3 × 30)

40 (3 × 50)   or   (4 × 40)

Paper 6

1. 37
  + 46
  ____

2. 72
  − 39
  ____

3. 36
  × 3
  ____

4. 2) 108

5–10 Complete the following bus timetable. Each bus takes the same amount of time to do the journey.

Bus	A	B	C
High Street	2:40	3:50	
Broad Lane		4:00	5:05
Market Place	2:55		
Kent Road	3:05		

Two shelves are 65 cm and 89 cm long.

11 What is their total length in metres?

12 What is the difference in their lengths in centimetres?

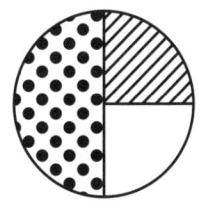

13 What fraction of the circle is spotted?

14 What fraction is striped?

15 What fraction is plain?

16 How many times larger is the spotted part than the striped part?

17–23 Complete the empty brackets in this multiplication table.

×	4	5	( )
	( )	10	( )
	12	( )	18
	( )	20	( )
	20	( )	

24 164 × 4 = _____

25 182 × 6 = _____

Put the correct sign in the spaces.

26–27 3 ____ 4 = 6 ____ 1

28–29 5 ____ 4 = 2 ____ 7

30–31 3 ____ 3 = 8 ____ 1

32–33 8 ____ 1 = 5 ____ 2

This **pictogram** shows how the children in Class 4 come to school.

Bus	👤👤👤👤👤
Walk	👤👤👤👤👤👤👤👤👤👤
Train	👤👤
Car	👤👤👤👤👤👤

Key

👤 = 1 child

34 How many children are there in the class? _____

35 How many more walk than come by car? _____

36 How many more come by car than by bus? _____

37 How many children don't come by bus? _____

38 How many more children walk than come by bus? _____

39 How many children don't come by train? _____

40 How many times can I take 9 from 54? _____

Paper 7

1. 345 ÷ 5 = _____
2. 345 + 456 = _____
3. 321 × 3 = _____

4–6 Fill in the missing numbers on this number line.

−7 _____ −5 _____ −3 _____ −1

7. Draw a circle around the highest temperature: −17 °C, −29 °C

8–12 Put these temperature in order, lowest first.

0 °C, −4 °C, −7 °C, 3 °C, −1 °C _____

13. My watch was 5 minutes fast. It showed 10:30. What was the right time? ____ : ____

Afternoon school begins at 1:30 and finishes at 3:35.

14. For how long do we work in the afternoon? ____ hr ____ min

15. What change should I have from £1.00 if I spent 67p? ____ p

16–20 Change this recipe for ginger nuts for 6 people to a recipe for 12 people for a party.

6 people	
125 g	flour
30 g	fat
75 g	sugar
30 ml	treacle
1 teaspoon	ground ginger

12 people	
____ g	flour
____ g	fat
____ g	sugar
____ ml	treacle
____ teaspoons	ground ginger

Underline the question in each line which does not have the same answer as the others.

21.   4 × 3   6 × 2   12 × 1   4 × 2

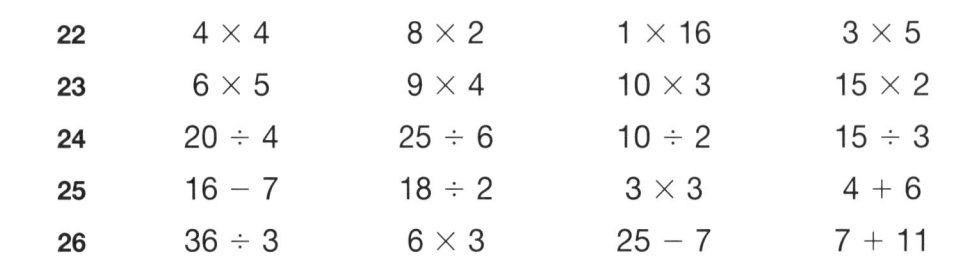

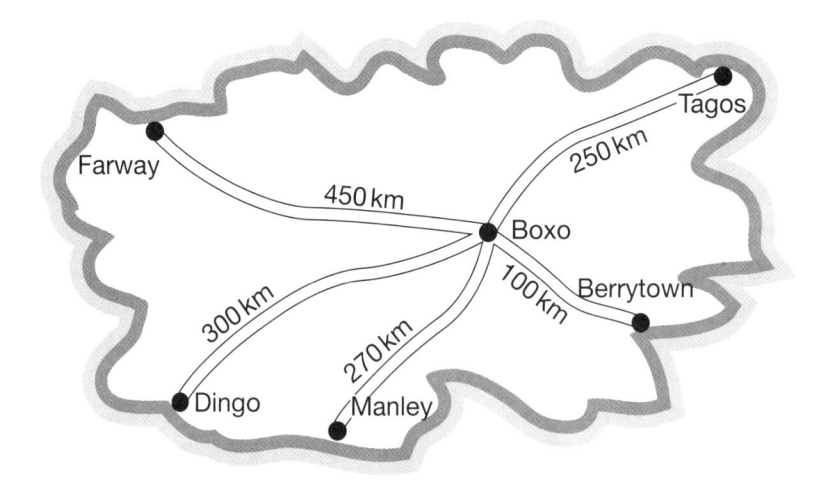

22	4 × 4	8 × 2	1 × 16	3 × 5
23	6 × 5	9 × 4	10 × 3	15 × 2
24	20 ÷ 4	25 ÷ 6	10 ÷ 2	15 ÷ 3
25	16 − 7	18 ÷ 2	3 × 3	4 + 6
26	36 ÷ 3	6 × 3	25 − 7	7 + 11

27 Which town is the furthest away from Boxo? _____

28 Which town is the nearest to Boxo? _____

29 How much further is it from Boxo to Farway than it is from Boxo to Manley? _____

30–31 Underline the smallest number and circle the largest.

5.7   4.8   7.5   8.4   4.5

32 Convert metres into centimetres: 7.45 m = _____ cm

33 **Round** to the nearest pound: £7.49 = £ _____

34 Convert centimetres into metres: 824 cm = _____ m

35 Write 345p in £.   345p = £ _____

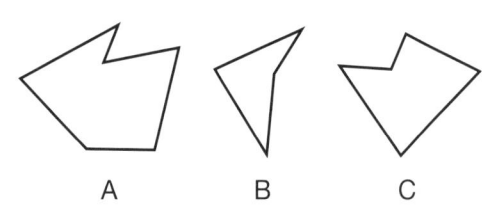

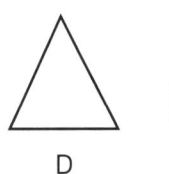

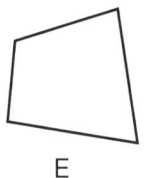

A   B   C   D   E

36–37 Shade in the **quadrilaterals** above.

A B C D E

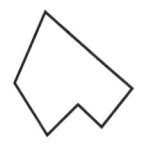

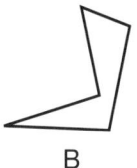

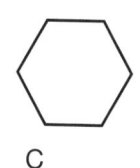

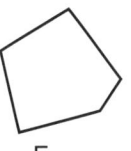

38–40 Shade in the **pentagons** above.

Now go to the Progress Chart to record your score! Total 40

Paper 8

1 How many pence in £1.25? _____

2 How many pence in £0.29? _____

A _____
B _____
C _____
D _____
E _____
F _____

3 Line A is _____ cm long.

4 Line B is _____ cm long.

5 Line C is _____ cm long.

6 Line D is _____ cm long.

7 Line E is _____ cm long.

8 Line F is _____ cm long.

9 What is the difference in length between the longest and the shortest line? _____ cm

10–11 Lines A and B put together would be the same length as lines _____ and _____ put together.

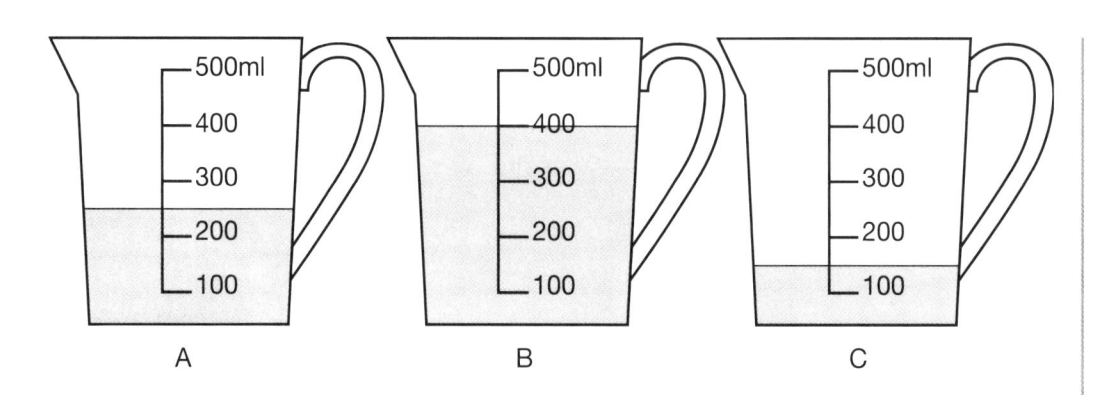

12–14 A has _____ ml.   B has _____ ml.   C has _____ ml.

How many ml of water would you have to add to each jug so that each one holds half a litre?

15–17 A needs _____ ml.   B needs _____ ml.   C needs _____ ml.

18 What is the remainder when 40 is divided by 6? _____

In the number 1234: how many tens are there?   3

how many hundreds are there?   2

19 In the number 135:   how many tens are there?   _____

20   how many hundreds are there?   _____

21 In the number 1247: how many units are there?   _____

22   how many hundreds are there?   _____

23 In the number 2439: how many tens are there?   _____

24   how many thousands are there?   _____

25 What is $\frac{1}{2}$ of 22? _____

26 $\frac{1}{3}$ of 24 is _____

27 $\frac{1}{4}$ of 20 is _____

28 What is $\frac{1}{5}$ of 15? _____

29 $\frac{1}{10}$ of 40 is _____

30 $\frac{1}{3}$ of 27 is _____

What are the names of these shapes?

Use the following words to help you:

sphere   triangular prism   **cuboid**   **cube**   cylinder

31 _____

32 _____

33 _____

34 _____

35 _____

36 John is 120.5 cm tall. James is 4.5 cm shorter.
How tall is James?   _____

37 What is the **area** of rectangle A?   _____ cm²

38 What is the **perimeter** of rectangle A?   _____ cm

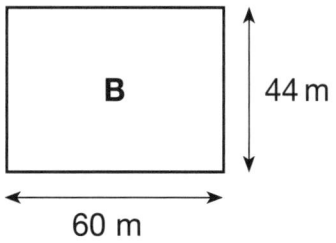

39 What is the **area** of rectangle B?   _____ m²

40 What is the **perimeter** of rectangle B?   _____ m

Now go to the Progress Chart to record your score!   Total   40

Paper 9

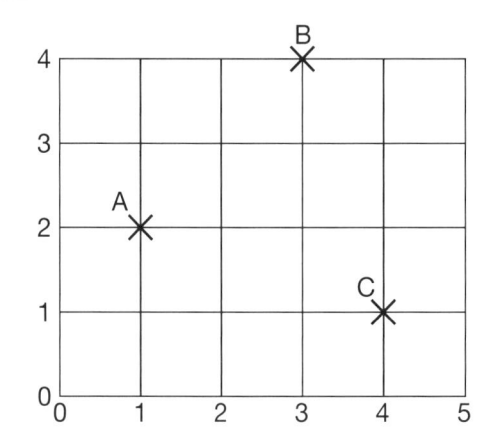

A is 1 square along and 2 squares up from (0,0).

1–2 B is _____ squares along and _____ squares up from (0,0).

3–4 C is _____ squares along and _____ square up from (0,0).

A is at the point (1,2).

5 B is at the point (_____, _____).

6 C is at the point (_____, _____).

7 D is at the point (2,3). Mark it on the grid above.

8 E is at the point (5,0). Mark it on the grid above.

9 4.9
   + 7.5
   _____

10 3.9
   × 8
   _____

11 Share 20 cherries among 5 children. They have _____ each.

12 How many glasses holding $\frac{1}{2}$ litre could be filled from a jug which holds $7\frac{1}{2}$ litres?

13 Sally missed the 9:25 a.m. bus. The next one is 17 minutes later. At what time is the next bus?

14 I had 9p after spending 24p. How much did I have at first?

15 Aziz walks 4 km each day. In November he walks _____ km.

Here is a bar chart which shows the number of hours of sunshine we had each day in the last week of June.

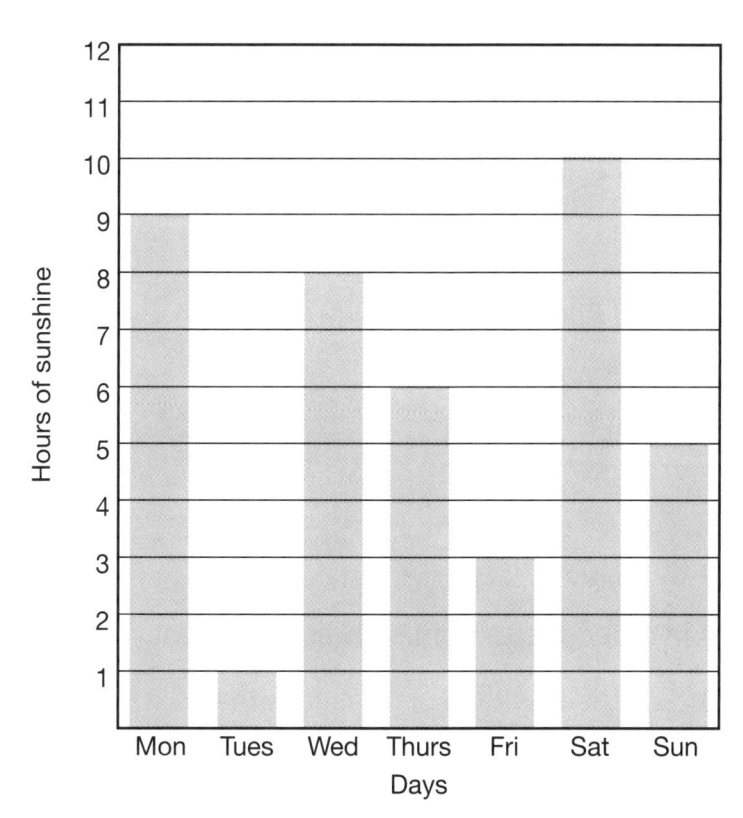

16–17 Which 2 days added together had the same amount of sunshine as Saturday?

_____ and _____

18 It rained on only one day in the week. On which day did it probably rain? _____

19–21 On which 3 days together did the total sunshine equal that of Monday?

_____ , _____ and _____

22 How many days had fewer than 6 hours of sunshine? _____

23 How many days had more than 8 hours of sunshine? _____

24 What was the total hours of sunshine for the week? _____

25–30 The sunniest day was Saturday. Write the other days in the order of sunniest day to least sunny day.

Saturday, _____ , _____ , _____ ,

_____ , _____ , _____ .

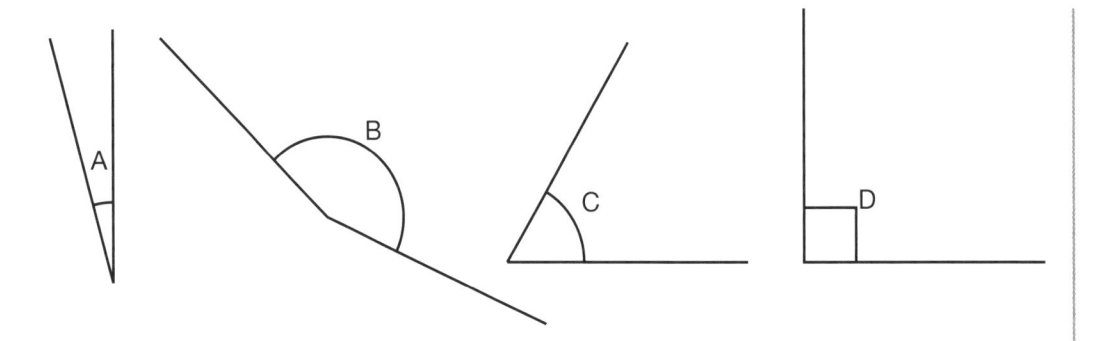

Look at the above angles and answer the following questions.

31 Which angle is the right angle? _____

32 The smallest angle is _____ .

33 The largest angle is _____ .

34 _____ is the 60° angle.

35–38 Place the angles in order of size from smallest to largest.

_____ is less than _____ is less than _____ is less than _____ .

39 Using the **digits** 5, 6 and 7 make as many 3-figure numbers as you can.

_____ _____ _____ _____ _____ _____

40 Now take away the smallest from the largest. _____

Now go to the Progress Chart to record your score! Total 40

Paper 10

1 Write the correct number in the box.

231 → ☐
   75 less is

2 Write the correct number in the box.

☐ → 260
   62 less is

24

3 Put these numbers in order, smallest to largest.

7536   6537   5736   6573

_____   _____   _____   _____

Look at this grid.

4 How many **squares** of this size are in the grid?

5 How many **squares** of this size are in the grid?

6 How many **squares** of this size are in the grid?

7 What is the total number of **squares** in the grid?

8 What is the smallest number you can make with these **digits**: 3, 5, 4, 9?

9 Now write it in words.

_____

10 What is the largest number you can make with these **digits**: 3, 5, 4, 9?

11 Now write it in words.

_____

12 What is the smallest number you can make with these **digits**: 9, 5, 8, 6, 1?

13 Now write it in words.

_____

14 What is the largest number you can make with these **digits**: 9, 5, 8, 6, 1? _____

15 Now write it in words.
_____

16 Write in figures one thousand, four hundred and eighty-nine. _____

17 Write in figures seven thousand and eighty-nine. _____

Here is a **pictogram** which shows what kind of books are liked most by children in Readwell School.

Key ☺ = 10 children

Mysteries	☺☺☺☺☺☺☺☺
Travel	☺☺☺☺
School Stories	☺☺☺☺☺☺☺☺☺
Books on Hobbies	☺☺☺
Animal Stories	☺☺☺☺☺☺☺

18 Which type of book is most popular? _____

19 Which type of book is least popular? _____

20 How many children are in the school? _____

21 Which kind of book is twice as popular as travel books? _____

22 How many more children like mysteries than animal stories? _____

23 How many more children prefer school stories to travel books? _____

Underline the right answer in each line.

24 **Round** £3.70 to the nearest pound: £3   £4   £7   £10   £70

25 **Round** £26.01 to the nearest pound: £20   £25   £26   £27   £30

26   £
   4.39
− 1.72
_____

27   £
   0.27
×   5
_____

26

Ring the correct answer.

28 When you add together two odd numbers the answer is:

   an odd number   an even number

29 If you add together two even numbers the answer is:

   an odd number   an even number

30 If you add together three even numbers the answer is:

   an odd number   an even number

31 If you add together three odd numbers the answer is:

   an odd number   an even number

32 What is the **sum** of the even numbers between 3 and 7? _____

33 What is the difference between 7 and 19? _____

34 How many times can I take £1.25 from £6.25? _____

Write the correct fraction in each space.

35 Shaded   _____
36 Unshaded _____

37 Shaded   _____
38 Unshaded _____

39 Shaded   _____
40 Unshaded _____

Now go to the Progress Chart to record your score!   Total   40

Paper 11

1. Sally left home at 08:52 and arrived at school at 09:01.

   How long did it take her to walk to school? _____

2. If I spent 23p and had 18p left, how much had I at first? _____ p

3. How many children are there altogether in a school if there are 197 boys and 165 girls? _____

Here are four regular pizzas. One whole, one cut in halves, one in thirds and one in sixths.

4. How many $\frac{1}{6}$s make 1 whole? _____

5. How many $\frac{1}{6}$s make $\frac{1}{3}$? _____

6. How many $\frac{1}{6}$s make $\frac{1}{2}$? _____

7. How many $\frac{1}{3}$s make 1 whole? _____

8. How many $\frac{1}{6}$s make $\frac{2}{3}$? _____

9. 369
    425
    + 264
    _____

10.   204
    × 8
    _____

11. How many times can I take 9 from 99? _____

12. From the **digits** 4, 5 and 6 make a number so that the 5 is the hundred and the 4 is the unit. _____

13. Write in figures two thousand and twenty. _____

14 How many times can I take 8 from 56? _____

15–17 Shade in the **hexagons**.

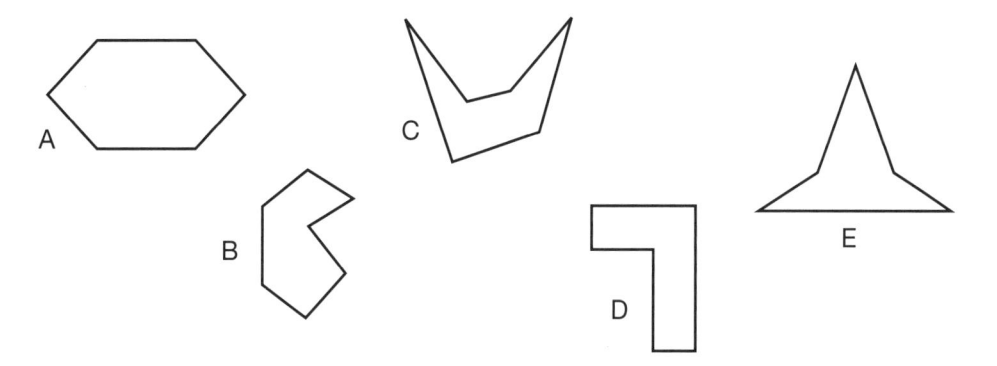

A B C D E

18–24 Here are the ingredients for a meal for 1 person.

Jacket Potato with Leeks and Cheese for 1 person	
1 large (about 200 g)	potato
10 g	butter
1 tablespoon	milk
2 (about 150 g)	leeks
40 g	grated cheese

Increase the measurements to change it to a recipe for 4 people.

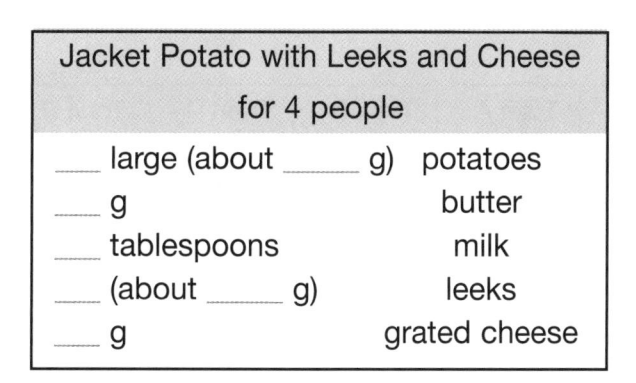

Jacket Potato with Leeks and Cheese for 4 people	
___ large (about ___ g)	potatoes
___ g	butter
___ tablespoons	milk
___ (about ___ g)	leeks
___ g	grated cheese

25–26 18 is half of _____, and three times as much as _____ .

27 How many jars of Bovo, each costing 75p, can I buy with £3.75? _____

This clock shows the correct time.

How fast or slow are the clocks below?

Write the number of minutes and ring the correct word for each clock.

28–29 _____ minutes   fast
                            slow

30–31 _____ minutes   fast
                            slow

32–33 _____ minutes   fast
                            slow

34–38 Each train takes 1 hr 10 min to reach Fordby. Write what time each one arrives.

	Train A	Train B	Train C	Train D	Train E
Leaves Bunmouth at	10:00	11:30	12:50	13:55	15:10
Arrives at Fordby at					

Put a sign in each space so that each question will be correct.

39   5 ___ 2 = 2 ___ 1

40   4 ___ 4 = 10 ___ 2

Now go to the Progress Chart to record your score!   Total   40

Paper 1 (pages 2–4)

1–6 Count the squares to find the area. Each triangle represents one half of a square and $\frac{1}{2} + \frac{1}{2} = 1$ whole; $\frac{1}{2}$ square + $\frac{1}{2}$ square + $\frac{1}{2}$ square + $\frac{1}{2}$ square = 2 wholes and so on.

1 **5** 4 squares + $\frac{1}{2}$ square + $\frac{1}{2}$ square = 5
2 **3** 2 squares + $\frac{1}{2}$ square + $\frac{1}{2}$ square = 3
3 **4** 2 squares + $\frac{1}{2}$ square + $\frac{1}{2}$ square + $\frac{1}{2}$ square + $\frac{1}{2}$ square = 4
4 **5** 4 squares + $\frac{1}{2}$ square + $\frac{1}{2}$ square = 5
5 **6**
6 **8** 6 squares + $\frac{1}{2}$ square + $\frac{1}{2}$ square + $\frac{1}{2}$ square + $\frac{1}{2}$ square = 8
7 **14** 2 × 7 = 14
8 **6** A face is a flat surface of a 3D shape.
9 **a square** Each face is the same length and width.
10 **6**
11 **a rectangle**
12–17 Subtract the minutes in the later time from the minutes in the earlier time to find the difference. For the questions that go into the next hour, count on from the first time to the next hour and then from the hour to the later time, and add the two results. 60 = 1hr
12 **11 minutes** 30 – 19 = 11
13 **23 minutes** 50 – 27 = 23
14 **20 minutes** 5:50 to 6:00 is 10 minutes and 6:00 to 6:10 is 10 minutes; 10 + 10 = 20
15 **9 minutes** 60 – 51 = 9
16 **39 minutes** 40 – 1 = 39
17 **18 minutes** 04:52 to 05:00 is 8 minutes and 05:00 to 5:10 is 10 minutes; 8 + 10 = 18
18 **71** Partition 20 into 20 and 9, then subtract from 100: 100 – 20 = 80; 80 – 9 = 71
19 **8** Use knowledge of the 7 times table to find the answer: 8 × 7 = 56, therefore 56 ÷ 7 = 8
20 **82** Use column addition. Begin by adding the digits on the right in the ones column. As 7 + 5 = 12, place the 2 in the ones column and the one beneath the lower line in the tens column. Then add the numbers in the tens column, including the 1 that has been carried over: 4 + 3 + 1 = 8.

```
    4 7
  + 3 5
  -----
    8 2
    1
```

21 **1** Two halves add up to one whole.

22–29 Negative numbers 'mirror' whole numbers, as shown in the diagram.

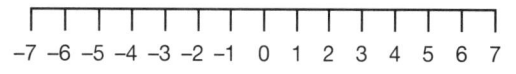

–7 –6 –5 –4 –3 –2 –1 0 1 2 3 4 5 6 7

22–23 **0, 2** 24–25 **–3, –1**
26–29 **–7, –5, –3, –1**
30–34 The year 2003 was before 2004, therefore if someone is born in 2003 they will be older than someone born in 2004. Knowledge of the order of months is needed as the same applies to the months of the year. For example, someone born in July will be older than someone born in August of the same year.
30–31 **David, Daley** 2003 is the earliest year shown so David is the eldest. Looking at the three birthdates in 2004, October is later in the year than April and July so Daley is the youngest.
32–34 **2, 2, David** The date is exactly 2 years after Maria was born. Anita turned 2 on 19 April 2006 (3 months before July). David turned 3 on 8 June 2006 (1 month before July).
35–37 Use knowledge of times tables.
35 **72**
36 **120** 6 × 2 = 12, so 6 × 20 = 120
37 **240** 6 × 4 = 24, so 6 × 40 = 240
38–40 Each number has a 0 in the ones place. Therefore the 0 just needs to be replaced with 5 each time: 0 + 5 = 5
38 **65** 39 **85** 40 **95**

Paper 2 (pages 4–7)

1–7 A is 9cm, B is 5.5cm, C is 5cm, D is 4cm, E is 8.5cm, F is 6.5cm and G is 9.5cm. A horizontal line goes from left to right, a vertical line goes up and down and a sloping line is diagonal.
1 **G** 2 **F** 3 **E**
4–5 Use column subtraction to find the difference. Make sure the larger number is at the top and the decimal points are lined up. Always work from right to left, as when subtracting a number without a decimal.

```
    8 . 5
  - 5 . 5
  -------
    3 . 0
```

4 **3** 3.0 is the same as 3, so either answer is acceptable.
5 **1.5** 6.5 – 5.0 = 1.5
6–7 Use column addition, making sure to add any numbers that are carried over. Make sure the decimal points are lined up and always work from right to left, as when adding a number without a decimal. Don't forget that 1 is the same as 1.0, so 3.5 + 1 is the same as 3.5 + 1.0

```
      6 . 5
+     5 . 0
    1 1 . 5
        ₁
```

6 **11.5** 5 + 6.5 = 11.5
7 **14** 5.5 + 8.5 = 14
8 **35** A product is found by multiplying numbers together: 3 × 7 = 35.
9 **28** Use column subtraction, making sure to borrow from the top number in the next column if the number being subtracted from is smaller.

```
   ⁵6  ¹0
 -  3   2
    2   8
```

10 **42p** Use column multiplication, making sure to work from right to left and add on any numbers carried over.

```
      1  4
  ×      3
      4  2
         ₁
```

11–20 Use a place value grid to help. In the number below, 7 thousands can be written as 7000, 4 hundreds can be written as 400 and 3 tens can be written as 30. The ones stay the same.

Thousands	Hundreds	Tens	Ones
7	4	3	2

11 **321**   12 **312**
13 **123**   14 **4000**
15 **900**   16 **40**
17 **4**   18 **9000**
19 **600**   20 **80**

21–22 **21, 27** First work out the difference between the numbers. 15 − 13 = 2, so the difference is 2: 19 + 2 = 21 and 25 + 2 = 27.
23 **89p** £1 is the same as 100p; 100 − 11 = 89. Refer to Q9 on using column subtraction.
24 **21p** 8 + 6 = 14; 14 + 7 = 21
25 **92** Refer to Paper 1 Q20 on column addition.
26 **35** Use 'short' division to complete the calculation. 3 does not go into 1, so write a zero above it and carry the 1 over to the next column to create the number 10. 3 goes into 10 three times, with a remainder of 1. Write 3 above the 10 and carry over the 1 to create the number 15. 3 goes into 15 five times, so write 5 above it.

```
      0  3  5
   3 │ 1 ¹0 ¹5
```

27 **20** Halving a number is the same as dividing by 2: 40 ÷ 2 = 20.
28 **100** When a number is divided by 10, it is moved one place to the right on a place value grid, as shown below.

Thousands	Hundreds	Tens	Ones	Decimal point	Tenths
1	0	0	0	.	
	1	0	0	.	0

29 **£76.00** Refer to Paper 1 Q20 on column addition. Calculate the price for 2 adults first (£22.50 + £22.50 = £45.00), then the price for 2 children (£15.50 + £15.50 = £31.00); finally add the 2 totals together (£45.00 + £31.00 = £76.00).
30 **£20.00** 4 × 5 = 20, so 4 × £5.00 = £20.00
31 **£6.40** Use column multiplication, making sure to work from right to left and add on any numbers carried over. Make sure the decimal points are lined up and complete the calculation as when multiplying a number without a decimal.

```
      1 . 6  0
  ×          4
      6 . 4  0
         ₂
```

32 **£102.40** Refer to Paper 2 Q6–7 on adding decimals. £76.00 + £20.00 + £6.40 = £102.40
33–34 **18, 17** Halve the total number of children (35 ÷ 2 = 17 remainder 1), then add the remainder to 17 (18 + 17 = 35).
35–38 There are 10 mm in 1 cm, therefore 25 mm = 2.5 cm. Use the ruler to count the number of centimetres or millimetres between each letter to find the answers.
35 **6 cm**
36 **2.5 cm or 25 mm**
37 **5.5 cm or 55 mm**
38 **3.5 cm or 35 mm**
39 **54** Write the question as a missing number sentence, then complete the inverse by multiplying the given numbers; ☐ ÷ 9 = 6 can be inverted to 6 × 9 = ☐ and 6 × 9 = 54.
40 **20** Refer to Paper 2 Q28 on dividing by 10. 200 ÷ 10 = 20

Paper 3 (pages 7–9)

1–6 Refer to Paper 1 Q1–6 on area.
1 **9**   2 **12**
3 **7**   4 **6**
5 **9** $\frac{1}{2}$ square + $\frac{1}{2}$ square = 1; 8 + 1 = 9
6 **7** 5 + $\frac{1}{2}$ + $\frac{1}{2}$ + $\frac{1}{2}$ + $\frac{1}{2}$ = 7
7 **25** If 2 weeks = 10 days, then 1 week = 5 days (10 ÷ 2 = 5) and 5 days × 5 weeks = 25.

8 **15** Find out how many lots of 4 hours go into 20 hours and multiply 3 days by the answer; 4 hours × 5 = 20 and 3 days × 5 = 15 days.
9 **6** Find out how many lots of 4 go into 24: 24 ÷ 4 = 6
10 **9** 1 magazine = 3 transfers, so multiply by 3: 3 × 3 = 9
11–15 **25, 40, 45, 60, 15** All numbers that can be divided by 5 will have the digits 0 or 5 in the ones place.
16 **seven thousand and one** Refer to Paper 2 Q11–20 on place value.
17–23 Always start at the location being looked **from**. For example, to find the direction of the school from the railway station, find the location of the railway station and look at the direction the school is from there.
17 **W**
18 **S**
19 **NW**
20 **NE**
21 **SE**
22 **S**
23 **SE**
24–27 To find the number halfway between, add the two numbers together and then divide by 2. Refer to Paper 2 Q26 on short division
24 **60** 50 + 70 = 120; 120 ÷ 2 = 60
25 **45** 35 + 55 = 90; 90 ÷ 2 = 45
26 **30** 25 + 35 = 60; 60 ÷ 2 = 30
27 **16** 12 + 20 = 32; 32 ÷ 2 = 16
28 **2005** If Jock is 3 years older, he was born 3 years before Jane; 2008 – 3 = 2005.
29 **2011** 2005 + 6 = 2011
30 **1999** 2011 – 11 = 1999. Refer to paper 2 Q9.
31–33

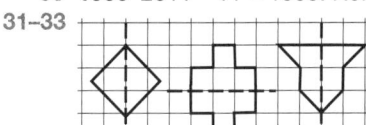

34–38 To find the largest number, place the digits in order from largest to smallest. Refer to Paper 2 Q11–20 on place value.
34 **8643**
35 **eight thousand, six hundred and forty-three**
36 **4320**
37 **four thousand, three hundred and twenty**
38 **3245**
39 **15** To find $\frac{1}{4}$ of a number, divide it by 4; 60 ÷ 4 = 15. Refer to Paper 2 Q29 on short division.
40 **25** 10:45 to 11:00 is 15 minutes and 11:00 to 11:10 is 10 minutes; 15 + 10 = 25.

Paper 4 (pages 10–12)

1 **206** Refer to Paper 1 Q20 on column addition.
2 **348** Refer to Paper 2 Q10 on column multiplication.
3 **£7.40** Refer to Paper 2 Q6–7 on adding decimals.
4–9 Work out the answer to the calculation that does not have any numbers missing first. Then complete the inverse of the other calculation. The inverse of multiplication is division and the inverse of addition is subtraction.
4 **4** 21 + 3 = 24; 24 ÷ 6 = 4
5 **7** 28 + 7 = 35; 35 ÷ 5 = 7
6 **12** 70 – 10 = 60; 60 ÷ 5 = 12
7 **3** 6 × 7 = 42; 45 – 42 = 3
8 **6** 6 × 9 = 54; 60 – 54 = 6
9 **23** 50 – 10 = 40; 40 – 17 = 23
10 **13** Add the numbers in the circle for 'Dogs': 10 + 3 = 13.
11 **14** Add the numbers in the circle for 'Cats': 3 + 11 = 14.
12 **3** Find the number in the overlap of the circles for 'Dogs' and 'Cats'.
13 **13** Add the numbers outside the circle for 'Dogs': 11 + 2 = 13.
14 **12** Add the numbers outside the circle for 'Cats': 10 + 2 = 12.
15 **26** Add all the numbers in the Venn diagram: 10 + 3 + 11 + 2 = 26.
16 **9** Write the question as a missing number sentence, then complete the inverse by subtracting: ☐ + 16 = 25 can be inverted to 25 – 16 = ☐ and 25 – 16 = 9.
17 **–1 °C** The black dots show the temperature and the last one is shown below –1 °C.
18 **–9 °C** Refer to Paper 1 Q22–29 on negative numbers. Numbers decrease in size as they move to the left on the number line, therefore –9 °C is lower than –7 °C.
19 **2001** 2010 – 9 = 2001
20 **Martin** 2007 is before 2008, therefore Martin is the elder.
21 **360** Find the total of each row and add the answers together. Remember that a whole 'stickman' represents 10 and half a 'stickman' represents 5. Farm Lane = 25; High Street = 100; Birch Avenue = 75; Riverside Road = 110; Manor Road = 50; 25 + 100 + 75 + 110 + 50 = 360.
22–29 Use your working out from question 21 to find the answers.
22 **Riverside Road**
23 **Manor Road** Divide the number on the High Street by 2 (100 ÷ 2 = 50); Manor Road has 50 children.
24 **Farm Lane** Divide the number on Birch Avenue by 3 (75 ÷ 3 = 25); Farm Lane has 25 children.

25–28

Farm Lane	👤	👤	👤							
High Street	👤	👤	👤	👤	👤	👤	👤	👤		
Birch Avenue	👤	👤	👤	👤	👤	👤	👤	👤	½	
Riverside Road	👤	👤	👤	👤	👤	👤	👤	👤	👤	½
Manor Road	👤	👤	👤	👤						

29 **380** 360 + 20 = 380
30 **14** Refer to Paper 2 Q9 on column subtraction; 33 − 19 = 14.
31 **92** Refer to Paper 1 Q20 on column addition: 77 + 15 = 92.
32 **78** Refer to Paper 2 Q10 on column multiplication: 3 × 26 = 78.
33 **1** There is only one shape with 4 right-angles and 4 equal sides.
34 **2** Remember that a square is a rectangle with 4 equal sides.
35 **12** 2 large triangles + 4 medium-sized triangles + 6 small triangles = 12 triangles
36 **60 − 5** 60 − 5 = 55; all the others = 50
37 **7 × 6** 7 × 6 = 42; all the others = 48
38 **299** 300 − 1 = 299
39 **280** 278 + 2 = 280
40 **96** 106 − 10 = 96

Paper 5 (pages 12–14)

1–3 Refer to Paper 1 Q22–29 on negative numbers.
1 **−8 °C**   2–3 **−2, 3**
4 **121** Use knowledge of the 11 times table.
5 **5** If 15 ÷ 3 = 5 then 150 ÷ 30 = 5 also. Alternatively, use repeated addition and count up in lots of 30.
6 **31** Refer to Paper 2 Q9 on using column subtraction.
7 **90 minutes** 1 hour = 60 minutes and $\frac{1}{2}$ hour = 30 minutes; 60 + 30 = 90 minutes
8 **1500 g** 1 kg = 1000 g and 0.5 kg = 500 g; 1000 + 500 = 1500 g
9 **102** Refer to Paper 2 Q26 on short division.
10 **1.5 m** 100 cm = 1 metre and 50 cm = 0.5 m; 1.0 + 0.5 = 1.5 m
11–12 The area of a rectangle can be found by multiply the length by the width. The perimeter of a rectangle can be found by adding up the 2 lengths and the 2 widths.
11 **21** 7 × 3 = 21
12 **20** 7 + 7 + 3 + 3 = 20
13 **51** Picture the shape as 2 rectangles, the original rectangle and a new rectangle 10 cm long and 3 cm high; find the area of the new rectangle (10 × 3 = 30) and add it to the area of the original rectangle to find the new total area (30 + 21 = 51).
14 **40** Refer to Paper 1 Q20 on column addition; 17 + 17 = 34 and 3 + 3 = 6; 34 + 6 = 40.
15–17 Add the first two numbers in the number sentence together, then subtract your answer from the answer shown in the equation.
15 **3** 3 + 4 = 7; 10 − 7 = 3
16 **2** 5 + 1 = 6; 6 − ☐ = 4; 6 − 4 = 2
17 **3** 3 + 3 = 6; 9 − 6 = 3
18–26 Use knowledge of the 7 and 6 times tables to help find the answer.
18–22 **49, 28, 56, 35, 77**
23–26 **36, 72, 96, 24**
27–32 Refer to Paper 2 Q35–38 on answering questions on length using a ruler.
27 **2 cm**
28 **0.5 cm or 5 mm**
29 **3.5 cm or 35 mm**
30 **4 cm**
31 **4 cm**
32 **2.5 cm or 25 mm**
33–36 If the numbers increase, the sequence is addition or multiplication. If they decrease, it is subtraction or division.
33–34 **36, 42** The sequence is to add 6; 30 + 6 = 36: 36 + 6 = 42.
35–36 **35, 32** The sequence is to subtract 3: 38 − 3 = 35; 35 − 3 = 32.
37–40 Work out the answer to each equation shown in the brackets and then compare the answers. Refer to Paper 2 Q10 on column multiplication.
37 **3 × 22** 6 × 10 = 60; 3 × 22 = 66; 66 is greater than 60.
38 **11 × 10** 5 × 20 = 100; 11 × 10 = 110; 110 is greater than 100.
39 **10 × 10** 10 × 10 = 100; 3 × 30 = 90; 100 is greater than 90.
40 **4 × 40** 3 × 50 = 150; 4 × 40 = 160; 160 is greater than 150.

Paper 6 (pages 15–16)

1 **83** Refer to Paper 1 Q20 on column addition.
2 **33** Refer to Paper 2 Q9 on column subtraction.
3 **108** Paper 2 Q10 on column multiplication.
4 **54** Paper 2 Q26 on short division.
5–10 Refer to Paper 1 Q12–17 on calculating time. Find the difference between the times in the columns. 3:50 to 4:00 is 10 min so add and subtract 10 min to find the times for the High Street and Broad Lane. 2:50 to 2:55 is 5 min, so add this to the times for Broad Lane to complete the row for the Market Place. 2:55 to 3:05 is 10 min, so add this to the times for the Market Place to complete the row for Kent Road.

Bus	A	B	C
High Street	2:40	3:50	**4:55**
Broad Lane	**2:50**	4:00	5:05
Market Place	2:55	**4:05**	**5:10**
Kent Road	3:05	**4:15**	**5:20**

11 **1.54 m or 154 cm** Refer to Paper 1 Q20 on column addition; 65 + 89 = 154; 100 cm is the equivalent of 1.00 m, so either answer is acceptable.
12 **24 cm** Refer to Paper 2 Q9 on column subtraction; 89 − 65 = 24.
13 $\frac{1}{2}$ **or** $\frac{2}{4}$ Imagine the circle is divided into 2 equal parts; 1 is dotted.
14 $\frac{1}{4}$ Imagine the circle is divided into 4 equal parts; 1 is striped.
15 $\frac{1}{4}$ Imagine the circle is divided into 4 equal parts; 1 is plain.
16 **twice** 2 quarters are the equivalent of $\frac{1}{2}$
17–23 5 × 2 = 10, so that row is multiplied by 2; 3 × 6 = 18, so that column is multiplied by 6 and so on.

×	4	5	**(6)**
2	**(8)**	10	**(12)**
3	12	**(15)**	18
4	**(16)**	20	**(24)**
5	20	**(25)**	30

24–25 Refer to Paper 2 Q10 on column multiplication.
24 **656** 25 **1092**
26–33 Begin by finding and noting the answer when the numbers on the left are added, subtracted, multiplied and divided. Then add, subtract, multiply and divide the numbers on the right to find an answer that matches.
26–27 **+, +** 3 + 4 = 6 + 1 = 7
28–29 **+, +** 5 + 4 = 2 + 7 = 9
30–31 **×, +** 3 × 3 = 8 + 1 = 9
32–33 **−, +** 8 − 1 = 5 + 2 = 7
34–39 Each 'stickman' represents 1 child, so 5 children catch the bus, 12 walk, 2 catch the train and 6 travel by car.
34 **25** 5 + 12 + 2 + 6 = 25
35 **6** 12 − 6 = 6   36 **1** 6 − 5 = 1
37 **20** 25 − 5 = 20 38 **7** 12 − 5 = 7
39 **23** 25 − 2 = 23
40 **6** This is the same as finding how many lots of 9 are in 54; 54 ÷ 9 = 6.

Paper 7 (pages 17–19)

1 **69** Refer to Paper 2 Q26 on short division.
2 **801** Refer to Paper 1 Q20 on column addition.
3 **963** Refer to Paper 2 Q10 on column multiplication.

4–12 Refer to Paper 1 Q22–29 on negative numbers.
4–6 **−6, −4, −2** 7 **−17 °C**
8–12 **−7 °C, −4 °C, −1 °C, 0 °C, 3 °C**
13 **10:25** Subtract 5 minutes from 30 minutes: 30 − 5 = 25 minutes.
14 **2 hr 5 minutes** 1:30 to 2:30 is 1 hour, 2:30 to 3:30 is 1 hour and 3:30 to 3:35 is 5 minutes; 1 hour + 1 hour + 5 minutes = 2 hours 5 minutes.
15 **33** Refer to Paper 2 Q9 on using column subtraction: £1.00 − £0.67 = £0.33 or 100 − 67 = 33.
16–20 2 × 6 = 12, so multiply each of the amounts shown by 2. Refer to Paper 2 Q10 on column multiplication.
16 **250** 2 × 125 = 250
17 **60** 2 × 30 = 60
18 **150** 2 × 75 = 150
19 **60** 2 × 30 = 60   20 **2** 2 × 1 = 2
21–26 Use knowledge of the times tables to complete the equations in each row. Invert the division equations to use the times tables, for example, 10 ÷ 2 = ☐ is the same as ☐ × 2 = 10
21 **4 × 2** 4 × 2 = 8; all the others = 12
22 **3 × 5** 3 × 5 = 15; all the others = 16
23 **9 × 4** 9 × 4 = 36; all the others = 30
24 **25 ÷ 6** 25 ÷ 6 = 4 remainder 1; all the others = 5
25 **4 + 6** 4 + 6 = 10; all the others = 9
26 **36 ÷ 3** 36 ÷ 3 = 12; all the others = 18
27 **Farway** 450 km is the greatest distance shown from Boxo.
28 **Berrytown** 100 km is the smallest distance shown from Boxo.
29 **180 km** Refer to Paper 2 Q9 on using column subtraction: 450 − 270 = 180.
30–31 **4.5, 8.4** Place the numbers in a grid, ensuring the decimal points are lined up. Look for the smallest number in the first column: If any numbers are the same, find the smallest number in the next column. Then look for the largest number in the first column; again, if any numbers are the same, find the largest number in the next column.

5	•	7
4	•	8
7	•	5
8	•	4
4	•	5

32 **745 cm** There are 100 cm in 1 metre, so multiply 7.45 by 100. To multiply by 100, place the numbers on a decimal grid using hundreds, tens, units, tenths, hundredths, thousandths, etc. To make a number larger, move the numbers to the left: 7.45 × 100 = 745

Hundreds	Tens	Ones	Decimal point	Tenths	Hundredths
		7	•	4	5
7	4	5	•		

33 **£7** When rounding an amount of money to the nearest pound, look at the number in the tenths (10ps) column. If it is 4 or below, leave the number in the units columns (pounds) unchanged. If it is 5 or above, raise the number in the units (pounds) column by one. The 0.4 in 7.49 rounds up to 7.00.

34–35 To divide by 100, place the numbers in a decimal grid using hundreds, tens, units, tenths, hundredths, thousandths etc. Reduce a number by 100 by moving it two places to the right.

34 **8.24 m** There are 100 cm in 1 metre, so divide by 100: 824 ÷ 100 = 8.24.

35 **£3.45** There are 100p in £1.00, so divide by 100: 345 ÷ 100 = 3.45.

36–37 **B and E shaded** A quadrilateral has 4 sides.

38–39 **B, D and E shaded** A pentagon has 5 sides.

Paper 8 (pages 19–21)

1–2 There are 100p in £1.00, so multiply the numbers by 100. Refer to Paper 7 Q32 on multiplying by 100.

1 **125** 1.25 × 100 = 125
2 **29** 0.29 × 100 = 29
3 **6.5**   4 **8**
5 **3**   6 **7.5**
7 **7**   8 **8.5**

9 **5.5** Refer to Paper 2 Q4–5 on subtracting decimals. 3 is the same as 3.0 and 8.5 – 3.0 = 5.5

10–11 **D, E** Refer to Paper 2 Q6–7 on adding decimals. 6.5 + 8 = 14.5 so subtract the length of each line from 14.5 and look for a line that is the same length as the answer; 14.5 – 7.5 = 7.0 and 7.0 + 7.5 = 14.5.

12–14 **250, 400, 150** If the measurement shown is halfway between two numbers, the answer will be halfway between those two numbers. For example, halfway between 100 and 200 is 150.

15–17 **250, 100, 350** Half a litre is 500 ml, so subtract the answers to Q12–14 from 500. Refer to Paper 2 Q9 on using column subtraction.

18 **4** Use knowledge of the 6 times table: 6 × 6 = 36 and 40 – 36 = 4.

19–24 Refer to Paper 2 Q11–20 on place value
19 **3**   20 **1**
21 **7**   22 **2**
23 **3**   24 **2**

25–30 To find a fraction of a number, divide the number by the denominator (the bottom number).
25 **11** 22 ÷ 2 = 11   26 **8** 24 ÷ 3 = 8
27 **5** 20 ÷ 4 = 5   28 **3** 15 ÷ 5 = 3
29 **4** 40 ÷ 10 = 4   30 **9** 27 ÷ 3 = 9

31 **cylinder** A cylinder has a curved face around the middle and a circular face at each end.

32 **cube** A cube has 6 square faces.

33 **cuboid** A cuboid has 6 rectangular faces.

34 **sphere** A sphere is the same shape as a ball.

35 **triangular prism** A triangular prism has 3 rectangular faces around the middle and a triangular face at each end.

36 **116 cm** Refer to Paper 2 Q4–5 on subtracting decimals: 120.5 – 4.5 = 116.0.

37–40 Refer to Paper 5 Q11–12 on area and perimeter.

37 **2400** Remove the zeros to times 6 × 4 = 24. Then put the two zeros back in the answer: 2400.

38 **200** 60 + 60 + 40 + 40 = 200

39 **2640** 4 × 60 = 240; 2400 + 240 = 2640

40 **208** 60 + 60 + 44 + 44 = 208

Paper 9 (pages 22–24)

1–2 **3, 4**   3–4 **4, 1**

5–8 When reading or plotting coordinates on a grid, use the saying "Along the corridor and up the stairs" to remember to go horizontal, then vertical.

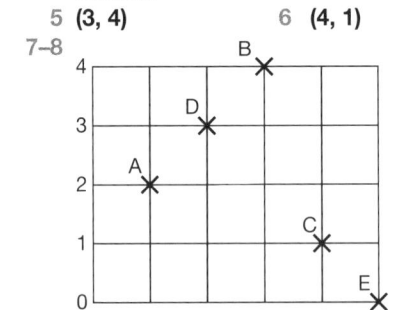

5 **(3, 4)**   6 **(4, 1)**

7–8

9 **12.4** Refer to Paper 2 Q6–7 on adding decimals.

10 **31.2** Refer to Paper 2 Q31 on multiplying decimal numbers.

11 **4** Refer to Paper 2 Q39 on completing the inverse. 20 ÷ 5 = ☐; ☐ × 5 = 20 and 4 × 5 = 20

12 **15** There are 2 halves in 1 whole, so there are 14 halves in 7 wholes; 14 halves + 1 half = 15 halves.

13 **9:42 a.m.** Add 17 onto the number of minutes shown in the time: 25 + 17 = 42 minutes, therefore the time will be 9:42. Refer to Paper 1 Q20 on column addition.

14 **33p** 24 + 9 = 33

15 **120 km** There are 30 days in November and 4 × 30 = 120.

16–30 The number that the top of the grey bar is level with shows the 'Hours of sunshine'. Monday had 9 hours, Tuesday had 1 hour, Wednesday

had 8 hours, Thursday had 6 hours, Friday had 3 hours, Saturday had 10 hours and Sunday had 5 hours.
16–17 **Monday, Tuesday** Saturday had 10 hours and 9 + 1 = 10
18 **Tuesday** As Tuesday had the least amount of sunshine, it is most likely to have rained that day.
19–21 **Tuesday, Friday, Sunday** There were 9 hours of sunshine on Monday and 1 + 3 + 5 = 9.
22 **3** There are 3 grey bars which are lower than the line showing 6 hours: Tuesday, Friday and Sunday.
23 **2** There are 2 grey bars which are higher than the line showing 8 hours: Monday and Saturday.
24 **42** 9 + 1 + 8 + 6 + 3 + 10 + 5 = 42
25–30 **Monday, Wednesday, Thursday, Sunday, Friday, Tuesday** Write the days with the largest number of hours of sunshine to the smallest.
31 **D** A right angle is 90°, like the corner of a square.
32 **A**
33 **B**
34 **C** This is the only angle that remains.
35–38 **A, C, D, B** Begin with the smallest angle and write them in increasing size.
39 **567, 576, 657, 675, 756, 765** Begin by writing a number starting with 5, then add the remaining numbers and swap them round (567 and 576), then repeat with numbers starting with 6 and 7.
40 **198** Refer to Paper 2 Q9 on using column subtraction: 765 – 567 = 198.

Paper 10 (pages 24–27)

1 **156** Refer to Paper 2 Q9 on using column subtraction: 231 – 75 = 156.
2 **322** Write as a missing number sentence and invert the calculation. Refer to Paper 1 Q20 on column addition. ☐ – 62 = 260 can be inverted to 62 + 260 = ☐ and 62 + 260 = 322
3 **5736, 6537, 6573, 7536** Place the numbers in a grid and find the smallest number in the first column. If any numbers in the column are the same, find the smallest number in the next column.

7	5	3	6
6	5	3	7
5	7	3	6
6	5	7	3

4 **1** The square is the same size as the outline of the grid.
5 **4**

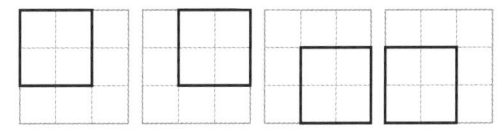

6 **9** Count the number of small squares in the grid.
7 **14** 1 + 4 + 9 = 14
8–13 To find the smallest number, place the digits in order from smallest to largest. To find the smallest number, write the digits in order from smallest to largest. To find the largest number, write the digits in order from largest to smallest. Use a place value grid, like the one shown in Paper 2 Q11–20. Refer to Paper 2 Q11–20 on place value.
8 **3459**
9 **three thousand four hundred and fifty-nine**
10 **9543**
11 **nine thousand five hundred and forty-three**
12 **15 689**
13 **fifteen thousand six hundred and eight-nine**
14 **98 651**
15 **ninety-eight thousand six hundred and fifty-one**
16 **1489**   17 **7089**
18–23 Each 'smiley face' represents 10 children, so 80 children like mystery books, 40 children like travel books, 90 children like school stories, 30 children like books on hobbies and 70 children like books on animal stories.
18 **school stories** The greatest number of children like school stories.
19 **books on hobbies** The smallest number of children like books on hobbies.
20 **310** 80 + 40 + 90 + 30 + 70 = 310
21 **mysteries** 40 children like travel books and 2 × 40 = 80
22 **10** 80 – 70 = 10
23 **50** 90 – 40 = 50
24–25 Refer to Paper 7 Q33 on rounding money.
24 **£4** 3 is rounded up to 4 as it is followed by 7
25 **£26** 6 remains the same as it is followed by 0
26 **£2.67** Refer to Paper 2 Q6–7 on adding decimals.
27 **£1.35** Refer to Paper 2 Q31 on multiplying decimal numbers.
28–31 An even number can be divided into 2 equal groups, so when 2 even numbers are added together the answer will be even. An odd number cannot be divided into 2 equal groups as there will always be 1 left over. Therefore two odd numbers will have 2 lots of 1 left over and 1 + 1 = 2, which is an even number. Three odd numbers will have 3 left over when separated equally and 1 + 1 + 1 = 3 and so on.
28 **an even number**   29 **an even number**
30 **an even number**   31 **an odd number**
32 **10** Add to find the sum: 4 + 6 = 10

33 **12** Subtract to find the difference: 19 − 7 = 12

35–40 Count the sections the shape has been divided into to find the denominator (lower number). Count the shaded sections to find the numerator (upper number) of the shaded part. Count the unshaded sections to find the numerator of unshaded part.

35 $\frac{1}{4}$ 36 $\frac{3}{4}$ 37 $\frac{1}{5}$

38 $\frac{4}{5}$ 39 $\frac{2}{3}$ 40 $\frac{1}{3}$

Paper 11 (pages 28–30)

1 **9 minutes** Refer to Paper 1 Q12–17 on calculating elapsed time. 08:52 to 09:00 is 8 minutes and 09:00 to 09:01 is 1 minute: 8 + 1 = 9.

2 **41** 23 + 18 = 41

3 **362** Refer to Paper 1 Q20 on column addition: 197 + 165 = 362.

4–8 Use the pictures of the pizzas to find the equivalent fractions. Equivalent fractions are fractions that are the same size, but written with different numbers. For example, $\frac{1}{2}$ is the same size as $\frac{2}{4}$.

4 **6** The fourth picture shows the whole pizza separated into sixths; 6 × $\frac{1}{6}$ = 1 whole.

5 **2** 2 sixths ($\frac{2}{6}$) are the same size as $\frac{1}{3}$.

6 **3** 3 sixths ($\frac{3}{6}$) are the same size as $\frac{1}{2}$.

7 **3** Count the number of thirds on the third pizza; 3 × $\frac{1}{3}$ = 1 whole.

8 **4** 4 sixths ($\frac{4}{6}$) are the same size as $\frac{2}{3}$.

9 **1058** Refer to Paper 1 Q20 on column addition.

10 **1632** Refer to Paper 2 Q10 on column multiplication.

11 **11** Use knowledge of times tables and use the inverse to find how many lots of 9 go into 99; 11 × 9 = 99 so 99 ÷ 9 = 11.

12–13 Refer to Paper 2 Q11–20 on place value.

12 **564**   13 **2020**

14 **7** Use knowledge of the times tables and use the inverse to find how many lots of 8 go into 56; 7 × 8 = 56 and 56 ÷ 8 = 7.

15–17 **A, C, D** A hexagon has 6 sides.

18–24 **4, 800, 40, 4, 8, 600, 160** The measurements shown are for 1 person, so multiply each measurement by 4 to find how much is needed for 4 people: 4 × 1 = 4; 4 × 200 = 800; 4 × 10 = 40; 4 × 1 = 4; 4 × 2 = 8; 4 × 150 = 600; 4 × 40 = 160

25–26 **36, 6** Multiply 18 by 2 to find the number which is half (18 × 2 = 36). Divide 18 by 3 to find the number it is 3 times as much as (18 ÷ 3 = 6).

27 **5** Use repeated addition to find the answer: 75p + 75p + 75p + 75p + 75p = 375p, which is the same as £3.75.

28–33 Moving around a clock face, each number represents 5 minutes that have passed. Use the numbers on the clock to count on or back in 5s. The correct time is 3:05 (the minute hand is pointing to the 1, so it is 5 minutes past; the hour hand is pointing to the 3). If a clock shows an earlier time than this then it is slow; if it shows a later time it is fast. Refer to Paper 1 Q12–17 on calculating elapsed time.

28–29 **5, fast** The time shown is 3:10; 3.05 to 3.10 is 5 minutes. 3:10 is later than 3:05.

30–31 **10, slow** The time shown is 2:55; 2:55 to 3:00 is 5 minutes and 3:00 to 3:05 is 5 minutes; 5 + 5 = 10. 2:55 is earlier than 3:05.

32–33 **20, slow** The time shown is 2:45; 2:45 to 3:00 is 15 minutes and 3.00 to 3:05 is 5 minutes; 15 + 5 = 20. 2:45 is before 3:05.

34 **11:10** 10:00 + 1 hour = 11:00 and 11:00 + 10 minutes = 11:10

35 **12:40** 11:30 + 1 hour = 12:30 and 12:30 + 10 minutes = 12:40

36 **14:00** 12:50 + 1 hour = 13:50 and 13:50 + 10 minutes = 14:00

37 **15:05** 13:55 + 1 hour = 14:55 and 14:55 + 10 minutes = 15:05

38 **16:20** 15:10 + 1 hour = 16:10 and 16:10 + 10 minutes = 16:20

39–40 Refer to Paper 6 Q26–33 on solving number sentences with missing signs.

39 **−, +** 5 − 2 = 2 + 1 = 3

40 **+, −** 4 + 4 = 10 − 2 = 8

Paper 12 (pages 31–33)

1–3 Refer to Paper 1 Q12–17 on calculating elapsed time. 30 min = 1.2 an hour; 15 min = $\frac{1}{4}$ of an hour.

1 **3:07 p.m.** 2:37 to 3:00 is 23 minutes; 30 − 23 = 7 minutes still to be added; 3:00 + 7 minutes = 3:07

2 **11:45 p.m.** 11 is the hour before midnight and 60 − 15 = 45.

3 **10:51** 45 + 6 = 51

4–10 Refer to Paper 2 Q6–7 on adding decimals and Paper 2 Q4–5 on subtracting decimals.

4–5 **A and D** 11.50 + 11.25 = 22.75; £22.75 is £0.25 less than £23.00 (all the other possible pairs add up to more than £23:00).

6 **£24.20** £11.25 + £12.95 = £24.20

7 **£1.50** £13.00 − £11.50 = £1.50

8 **£1.75** £15.00 − £13.25 = £1.75

9 **£61.70** £11.50 + £13.25 + £12.75 + £11.25 + £12.95 = £61.70

10 **£34.00** £11.25 + £11.25 = £22.50; £11.50 + £22.50 = £34.00

11–14 The line of symmetry creates a mirror image on each side of the shape.

11

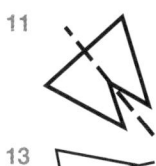

12

13

14

15–26 Start with the time given and add to work out the other times. For example, the question states that the first lesson begins at 09:30 and each lesson is half an hour long, so the first lesson ends at 10:00. The time that a lesson ends is the same time as the start of the next lesson.

	Begins	Ends
First lesson	09:30	10:00
Second lesson	10:00	10:30
Break	10:30	10:45
Third lesson	10:45	11:15
Fourth lesson	11:15	11:45
Fifth lesson	11:45	12:15

27 **A – iii** A cube has 6 faces which are all the same size.
28 **B – i** Each face shown on the pyramid is triangular.
29 **C – ii** The length of the longer sides is shown as the same length as two squares on the net.
30 **D – iv** The pyramid has a square base, so this must be shown on one side of the net. As it is a pyramid, the rest of the faces will be triangular.
31 **150 ml** Refer to Paper 2 Q9 on using column subtraction: 1 litre = 1000 ml and 1000 − 850 = 150.
32–38 The key shows that 1 'stickman' represents 2 children and half a 'stickman' represents 1 child. Therefore, there 2 × 2 = 4 children aged 7; 4 × 2 = 8 children aged 8; 7 × 2 = 14 and 14 + 1 = 15 children aged 9; 9 × 2 = 18 children aged 10; 8 × 2 = 16 and 16 + 1 = 17 children aged 11.
32 **62** 4 + 8 + 15 + 18 + 17 = 62
33 **10** 18 − 8 = 10
34 **group A** 18 + 17 = 35 children in Group A; 4 + 8 + 15 = 27 children in Group B
35 **8** 35 − 27 = 8
36 **£930** Partition £15.00 into £10.00 and £5.00: 62 × £10 = £620 and 62 × £5 = £310; £620 + £310 = £930
37 **37** 18 + 17 = 35 and 35 + 2 = 37
38 **25** 62 − 37 = 25
39 **3** 5 × 5 = 25 and 28 − 25 = 3
40 **4** 4 × 6 = 24 and 28 − 24 = 4

Paper 13 (pages 34–36)

1–14 Subtract the first number shown in each missing number sentence from the answer. Then find two numbers from each set of brackets that add up to the same number.
1–2 **1, 2** 12 − 9 = 3 and 1 + 2 = 3
3–4 **1, 3** 12 − 8 = 4 and 1 + 3 = 4
5–6 **2, 3 or 1, 4** 12 − 7 = 5; 2 + 3 = 5 and 1 + 4 = 5
7–8 **1, 4 or 2, 3** The combination not used in Q5–6.
9–10 **1, 5 or 2, 4** 12 − 6 = 6; 1 + 5 = 6 and 2 + 4 = 6
11–12 **2, 4 or 1, 5** The combination not used in Q9–10.
13–14 **3, 4** 12 − 5 = 7 and 3 + 4 = 7
15–18 Begin by completing the column with 9 in as only 1 and 2 can be added to 9 to make 12. Try placing the 1 or 2 in the top left circle and work through the rest of the calculations until they all add up to 12.

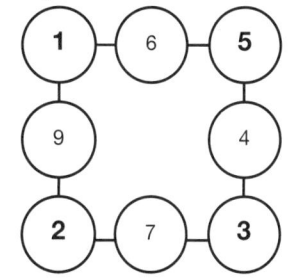

19–23 Use the squares to make sure the angles are reflected correctly.

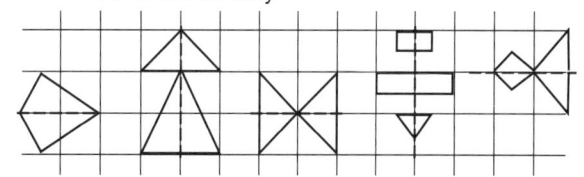

24–29 Refer to Paper 6 Q26–33 on solving number sentences with missing signs.
24 **+, × or ÷, −** 6 + 6 = 4 × 3 = 12 or 6 ÷ 6 = 4 − 3 = 1
25 **+, ×** 4 + 5 = 3 × 3 = 9
26 **−, + or ÷, ×** 6 − 2 = 3 + 1 = 4 or 6 ÷ 2 = 3 × 1 = 3
27 **−, −** 7 − 4 = 4 − 1 = 3
28 **−, + or ÷, −** 8 − 2 = 5 + 1 = 6 or 8 ÷ 2 = 5 − 1 = 4
29 **+, +** 7 + 1 = 4 + 4 = 8
30–35 The number that the top of the grey bar is level with shows the number of passengers who got on the bus at each stop: 7 at the crossroads, 3 at the railway, 10 at the hospital and 4 at Shaw Street.
30 **24** 7 + 3 + 10 + 4 = 24   31 **7** 10 − 3 = 7
32 **3** 7 − 4 = 3   33 **1** 4 − 3 = 1
34 **£14.40** Refer to Paper 2 Q10 on column multiplication and Paper 7 Q32 on multiplying

by 10; 24 × 6p = 144p, which is the same as £1.44 and £1.44 × 10 = £14.40.

35 **21** Find $\frac{1}{4}$ of 24 (24 ÷ 4 = 6) and subtract this from the total number of passengers (24 − 6 = 18), then add on the 3 new passengers (18 + 3 = 21).

36–37 **Mr Bell, Mr Eliot** 16 kg is the same as 16.0 kg; 8.6 and 14.8 are both less than 16.0.

38 **Mr Dring**

39 **5.4 kg** Refer to Paper 2 Q4–5 on subtracting decimals: 21.4 − 16.0 = 5.4

40 **7.4 kg** 16.0 − 8.6 = 7.4

Paper 14 (pages 36–38)

1–10 Refer to Paper 5 Q33–36 on sequences.

1–2 **95, 90** The sequence is to subtract 5: 100 − 5 = 95; 95 − 5 = 90

3–4 **43, 47** The sequence is to add 4: 39 + 4 = 43; 43 + 4 = 47

5–6 **523, 518** The sequence is to subtract 5: 528 − 5 = 523; 523 − 5 = 518

7–8 **237, 243** The sequence is to add 6: 231 + 6 = 237; 237 + 6 = 243

9–10 **110, 121** The sequence is to add 11: 99 + 11 = 110; 110 + 11 = 121

11 **14** Refer to Paper 2 Q26 on short division: 98 ÷ 7 = 14

12 **132** Use knowledge of the 11 or 12 times tables: 12 × 11 = 132

13 **20** 40 ÷ 2 = 2, so 400 ÷ 20 = 20

14 **12** Refer to Paper 2 Q9 on using column subtraction: 101 − 89 = 12

15 **30 minutes** 1 hour is 60 minutes and $\frac{1}{2}$ of 60 is 30

16 **2800** 7 × 4 = 28, so 70 × 40 = 2800

17 **201** Refer to Paper 2 Q26 on short division: 603 ÷ 3 = 201

18 **11:04** Add on 5 minutes to get to 11:00, then add the remaining 4 minutes (5 + 4 = 9)

19 **13** 21 − ☐ = 8 can be inverted to 21−2013 × 8 = ☐ as they are part of the same number family: 21 − 8 = 13.

20 **180** Refer to Paper 1 Q20 on column addition.

21 **28210** Refer to Paper 2 Q10 on column multiplication. As the number is being multiplied by 70, add a zero as the first digit on the right-hand side, then multiply each digit in 403 by 7.

22–27 Refer to Paper 5 Q11–12 on calculating area and perimeter.

22 **600** 2 × 3 = 6, so 200 × 3 = 600

23 **406** 200 + 200 + 3 + 3 = 406

24 **6000** 200 × 3 = 600, so 200 × 30 = 6000

25 **460** 200 + 200 + 30 + 30 = 460

26 **10** 6000 ÷ 600 = 10

27 **54 m** Refer to Paper 2 Q9 on using column subtraction: 460 − 406 = 54

28 **978** Refer to Paper 2 Q11–20 on place value; 7 must be in the tens column.

29 **1000** A product is found by multiplying numbers together. Refer to Paper 7 Q32 on multiplying by 100; 10 × 100 = 1000.

30–33 Use knowledge of times tables. The first number in each question has been partitioned in the second part of the number sentence. For example, in the calculation 12 × 7, the number 12 can be partitioned into 10 and 2; 10 × 7 = 70 and 2 × 7 = 14; 70 + 14 = 84.

30 **96** 10 × 8 = 80 and 2 × 8 = 16; 80 + 16 = 96

31 **105** 10 × 7 = 70 and 5 × 7 = 35; 70 + 35 = 105

32 **90** 10 × 5 = 50 and 8 × 5 = 40; 50 + 40 = 90

33 **144** 10 × 9 = 90 and 6 × 9 = 54; 90 + 54 = 144

34 **7** Find the total number of yellow and green counters (18 + 15 = 33) and subtract the answer from 40 (40 − 33 = 7).

35 **12** Find how many times 6 will go into 72; 72 ÷ 6 = 12.

36 **6** There are 100 centimetres in a metre. Use repeated addition to find how many lots of 15 go into 100: 15 + 15 + 15 + 15 + 15 + 15 = 90

37 **10 cm or 0.1 m** 100 − 90 = 10

38 **25** 1 + 3 + 5 + 7 + 9 = 25

39 **2000** All the digits are the same, except the one in the thousands place which has been increased by 2. Therefore 2000 has been added.

40 **500** All the digits are the same, except the one in the hundreds place which has been decreased by 5. Therefore 500 has been subtracted.

Paper 15 (pages 38–40)

1–2 **−20, −18** Refer to Paper 1 Q22–29 on negative numbers.

3 **4** There are 7 days in 1 week and 28 ÷ 7 = 4

4–6 Refer to Paper 2 Q35–38 on answering questions on length using a ruler.

4 **1 cm**   5 **2 cm**   6 **3 cm**

7 **1.5 cm or 15 mm** 23.5 to 24 is 0.5 cm (or 5 mm); 24 to 25 is 1 cm (or 10 mm); 0.5 + 1 = 1.5 cm (or 15 mm)

8 **1.5 cm or 15 mm** 20 to 21 is 1 cm (or 10 mm); 21 to 21.5 is 0.5 cm (or 5 mm); 1 + 0.5 = 1.5 cm (or 15 mm)

9 **7 cm**   10 **5 cm**   11 **2 cm**

12–14 To round numbers, look at the digit to the right of the number being rounded to. Round down if it is 4 or less and round up if it is 5 or more.

12 **200** 1 is rounded up to 2 as it is followed by 5.

13 **200** As 9 is in the tens place, this becomes 0 and the 1 is rounded up to 2.

14 **390** 197 + 197 = 394; 4 is rounded down to 0.

15–17 **B, C, E** A quadrilateral is a shape with 4 sides.

18 **126** A product is found by multiplying numbers together. 20 × 6 = 120 and 1 × 6 = 6; 120 + 6 = 126
19 **4** 16 ÷ 2 = 8 and 8 ÷ 2 = 4
20 **18** 2 × 9 = 18
21 **27** Add all the numbers in the Venn diagram; 11 + 5 + 8 + 3 = 27.
22 **13** Add all the numbers in the circle for 'Grey socks'; 5 + 8 = 13.
23 **16** Add all the numbers in the circle for 'Black shoes'; 11 + 5 = 16.
24 **5** Find the number in the overlap of the circles for 'Grey socks' and 'Black shoes'.
25 **11** Add the numbers outside the circle for 'Black shoes': 8 + 3 = 14.
26 **14** Add the numbers outside the circle for 'Grey shoes': 11 + 3 = 1.
27 **73** £1.00 is the same as 100p. Refer to Paper 2 Q9 on using column subtraction: 100 − 27 = 73
28–35 5 to 8 can also be written as 7:55. Refer to Paper 11 Q28–33 on telling the time and Paper 1 Q12–17 on calculating elapsed time.
28 **10, fast** The time shown is 8:05; 7:55 to 8:00 is 5 minutes and 8:00 to 8:05 is 5 minutes; 5 + 5 = 10. 8:05 is later than 7:55.
30 **20, slow** The time shown is 7:35; 7:35 to 7:55 is 20 minutes. 7:35 is earlier than 7:55.
32 **20, fast** The time shown is 8:15; 7:55 to 8:00 is 5 minutes and 8:00 to 8:15 is 15 minutes; 5 + 15 = 20. 8:15 is later than 7:55.
34 **30, slow** The time shown is 7:25; 7:25 to 7:55 is 30 minutes. 7:25 is earlier than 7:55.
36 **600** All the digits are the same, except the one in the hundreds place which has been decreased by 6. Therefore 600 has been subtracted.
37 **30** All the digits are the same, except the one in the tens place which has been increased by 3. Therefore 30 has been added.
38–40 Refer to Paper 2 Q11–20 on place value.
38 **86 552** Place the digits in order from largest to smallest.
39 **eighty-six thousand five hundred and fifty-two**
40 **4120**

Paper 16 (pages 41–44)

1–3 $\frac{1}{2}, \frac{3}{6}, \frac{6}{12}$ 6 out of 12 squares are shaded, which is $\frac{6}{12}$; $\frac{6}{12}$ is the equivalent of $\frac{1}{2}$ and $\frac{3}{6}$.
4–5 $\frac{1}{3}, \frac{2}{6}$ 1 group out of 3 has been circled, which is $\frac{1}{3}$, and 2 paperclips out of 6 have been circled which is $\frac{2}{6}$.
6 $\frac{1}{2}$ $\frac{1}{2}$ is the equivalent of $\frac{2}{4}$ and $\frac{2}{4}$ is larger than $\frac{1}{4}$.
7–8 The first two digits after a decimal point can be written as a fraction with a denominator of 100. For example, 0.75 is the same as $\frac{75}{100}$. Don't forget that 0.1 is the same as 0.10, 0.2 is the same as 0.20 and so on. Fractions can be simplified by dividing both numbers by the same number: both numbers in the fraction $\frac{75}{100}$ can be divided by 25; 75 ÷ 25 = 3 and 100 ÷ 25 = 4 which simplifies the fraction to $\frac{3}{4}$.
7 $\frac{1}{4}$ 0.25 is the same as $\frac{25}{100}$; 25 ÷ 25 = 1 and 100 ÷ 25 = 4 which simplifies the fraction to $\frac{1}{4}$
8 $\frac{1}{10}$ 0.1 is the same as 0.10, which can be written as $\frac{10}{100}$; 10 ÷ 10 = 1 and 100 ÷ 10 = 10 which simplifies the fraction to $\frac{1}{10}$
9 **6.50** Partition 13 into 10 and 3 and multiply 50p by both numbers (10 × 50p = 500p and 3 × 50p = 150p), then add the two answers together (500p + 150p = 650p = £6.50).
10 **Brighton** 280 km is the greatest distance shown.
11 **Cambridge** 135 km is the smallest distance shown.
12–13 Refer to Paper 2 Q9 on using column subtraction.
12 **27 km** 280 − 253 = 27
13 **95 km** 245 − 150 = 95
14–15 Refer to Paper 15 Q13–14 on rounding to the nearest 10.
14 **250 km** The 3 in 253 rounds down to 250.
15 **150 km** This is already rounded to the nearest 10 as the digit in the ones place is 0.
16 **8018** Refer to Paper 2 Q11–20 on place value.
17–19 Refer to Paper 11 Q28–33 on telling the time.
20–22 Refer to Paper 8 Q25–30 on finding a fraction of a number.
20 **13** 26 ÷ 2 = 13
21 **14** Find $\frac{1}{3}$ of 21 and then multiply the answer by 2 to find $\frac{2}{3}$: 21 ÷ 3 = 7 and 2 × 7 = 14.
22 **12** Find $\frac{1}{4}$ of 16 and then multiply the answer by 3 to find $\frac{3}{4}$: 16 ÷ 4 = 4 and 3 × 4 = 12.
23 **4.80** 6 × 8 = 48 so 6 × 80 = 480; 480p is the same as £4.80.
24 **5.10** Partition the number 85 into 80 and 5 and multiply them both by 6 (6 × 80 = 480 and 6 × 5 = 30), then add the answers together (480 + 30 = 510p = £5.10).
25 **4** Refer to Paper 1 Q20 on column addition and use repeated addition to find the answer: 45 + 45 + 45 + 45 = 180.
26–29 Refer to Paper 2 Q6–7 on adding decimals and Paper 2 Q4–5 on subtracting decimals. Don't forget that 39 is the same as 39.0.

26 **76.5** 39.0 + 37.5 = 76.5
27 **1.5** 39.0 − 37.5 = 1.5
28 **79.2** 37.5 + 41.7 = 79.2
29–33 The number that the top of the grey bar is level with shows the number of children; the numbers along the bottom show how tall they are. 1 child is 137 cm, 3 children are 138 cm, 5 children are 139 cm, 8 children are 140 cm, 4 children are 141 cm, 7 children are 142 cm, 0 children are 143 cm and 2 children are 144 cm.
29 **30** 1 + 3 + 5 + 8 + 4 + 7 + 2 = 30
30 **0**
31 **5** 8 − 3 = 5
32 **9** 1 + 3 + 5 = 9
33 **13** 4 + 7 + 2 = 13
34–37 There are 100 centimetres in a metre. Convert the measurements to centimetres to make the calculation easier, then divide the answer by 100 to change it back into metres. Refer to Paper 1 Q20 on column addition. To divide by 100, place the numbers in a decimal grid using hundreds, tens, units, tenths, hundredths, thousandths etc. Reduce a number by 100 moving it two places to the right.
34 **10 m** 4 m 25 cm = 425 m and 5 m 75 cm = 575 cm; 425 + 575 = 1000; 1000 ÷ 100 = 10
35 **16.04 m** 8 m 36 cm = 836 cm and 7 m 68 cm = 768 cm; 836 + 768 = 1604; 1604 ÷ 100 = 16.04
36 **2.55 m** 5 m 0 cm = 500 cm and 2 m 45 cm = 245 cm; 500 − 245 = 255; 255 ÷ 100 = 2.55
37 **3.40 m** 6 m 10 cm = 610 cm and 2 m 70 cm = 270 cm; 610 − 270 = 340; ÷ 100 = 3.40
38 **£1.20** Divide £6.00 by 5 to find the cost of 1 m. Refer to Paper 2 Q26 on short division. Place the decimal in the correct position in the answer space before beginning and complete the calculation as normal. 6.00 ÷ 5 = 1.20
39 **£13.20** Partition 11 into 10 and 1 and multiply 1.20 by each number (10 × 1.20 = 12.00 and 1 × 1.20 = 1.20), then add the answers together (12.00 + 1.20 = 13.20).
40 **5** There are 30 minutes in $\frac{1}{2}$ hour. Refer to Paper 1 Q12–17 on calculating elapsed time.

Paper 17 (pages 44–46)

1 **61** 30 + 31 = 61
2 **61** 31 + 30 = 61
3 **60** 29 + 31 = 60
4 **3** 31 − 28 = 3
5 **4** There are 12 months in 1 year; 48 ÷ 12 = 4
6 **1000** A millenium means 1000 years.
7 $\frac{1}{2}$ Imagine the square is divided into 8 equal rectangles; 1 is dotted.
8 $\frac{1}{2}$ Imagine the square is divided into 2 equal rectangles; 1 is striped.
9 $\frac{1}{8}$ Imagine the square is divided into 8 equal rectangles; 1 is plain.
10 $\frac{1}{4}$ Imagine the square is divided into 4 equal squares; 1 has crosses.
11 **66** Find the cost of one pencil by dividing by 3 (99 ÷ 3 = 33), then multiply the answer by 2 (33 × 2 = 66).
12 **42** A product is found by multiplying numbers together: 7 × 6 = 42.
13 **£5.50** Refer to Paper 2 Q26 on short division. Place the decimal in the correct position in the answer space before beginning and complete the calculation as normal: 66.00 ÷ 12 = 5.50
14–29 Refer to Paper 6 Q26–33 on solving number sentences with missing signs.
14–15 **+, +** 7 + 1 = 4 + 4 = 8
16–17 **+, ×** 3 + 7 = 5 × 2 = 10
18–19 **+, −** 6 + 1 = 8 − 1 = 7
20–21 **×, ×** 6 × 4 = 2 × 12 = 24
22–23 **×, +** 4 × 4 = 10 + 6 = 16
24–25 **÷, ÷** 12 ÷ 3 = 8 ÷ 2 = 4
26–27 **×, −** 2 × 7 = 15 − 1 = 14
28–29 **× or ÷, −** 3 × 1 = 3 or 3 ÷ 1 = 3 and 7 − 4 = 3
30–31 Refer to Paper 2 Q31 on multiplying decimals.
30 **2996**   31 **19.74**   32 **22.68**
33–40 Find the fractions to be compared in the grid and use it to count on and find the correct number.
33 **3**   34 **8**
35 **2**   36 **12**
37 **4**   38 **6**
39 **10** 40 **2**

Paper 18 (pages 46–48)

1–12 Refer to Paper 5 Q33–36 on sequences.
1–2 **£0.75 or 75p, £0.50 or 50p** The sequence is to subtract £0.25; £1.00 − £0.25 = £0.75; £0.75 − £0.25 = £0.50
3–4 **54p, 60p** The sequence is to add 6p: 48p + 6p = 54p; 54p + 6p = 60p.
5–6 **2055, 2065** The sequence is to add 10: 2045 + 10 = 2055; 2055 + 10 = 2065.
7–8 **2$\frac{1}{2}$, 3** The sequence is to add $\frac{1}{2}$: 2 + $\frac{1}{2}$ = 2$\frac{1}{2}$; 2$\frac{1}{2}$ + $\frac{1}{2}$ = 3.
9–10 **8 hr, 4 hr** 1 day = 24 hours. The sequence is to subtracr 4 hr: 12 hr − 4 hr = 8 hr; 8 hr − 4 hr = 4 hr.
11–12 **164, 172** The sequence is to add 8: 156 + 8 = 164; 164 + 8 = 172.
13–15 Refer to Paper 2 Q6–7 on adding decimals.
13 **41.1**   14 **63**   15 **82.7**
16–20 Invert the calculations to find the answer: addition is the inverse of subtraction and multiplication is the inverse of division.
16 **3** 12 ÷ 4 = 3

17 **6** 2 + 3 = 5; 11 − 5 = 6
18 **30** 5 × 6 = 30
19 **4** 12 − 8 = 4
20 **6** 30 − 24 = 6
21 **5** There are 12 months in 1 year and 60 ÷ 12 = 5.
22–23 Refer to Paper 2 Q6–7 on adding decimals and Paper 2 Q4–5 on subtracting decimals.
  22 **6.55** 4.75 + 1.80 = 6.55
  23 **3.45** 10.00 − 6.55 = 3.45
  24 **640** 2 × 32 = 64 so 20 × 32 = 640
  25 **84** A product is found by multiplying numbers together; 7 × 12 = 84.
26–29 Refer to Paper 2 Q10 on column multiplication.
  26 **56** 14 × 4 = 56   27 **84** 21 × 4 = 84
  28 **64** 16 × 4 = 64   29 **92** 23 × 4 = 92
30–34 Use knowledge of times tables to complete the inverse of the calculation and refer to Paper 2 Q26 on short division.
  30 **9** 54 ÷ 6 = 9   31 **6** 36 ÷ 6 = 6
  32 **7** 42 ÷ 6 = 7   33 **25** 150 ÷ 6 = 25
  34 **31** 186 ÷ 6 = 31
  35 **137** Refer to Paper 2 Q26 on short division. £6.85 is the same as 685p and 685p ÷ 5p = 137.
36–37 Work out the answer to the calculation on the left first, then subtract a number from the calculation on the right so they both have the same answer.
  36 **10** 50 × 1 = 60 − 10 = 50
  37 **7** 20 × 0 = 7 − 7 = 0
38–40 Refer to Paper 11 Q28–33 on telling the time.

Paper 19 (pages 48–50)

1–4 Refer to Paper 10 Q3 ordering numbers.
1–2 **£0.02, £2.22** Convert the amounts shown in pounds into pence: £2 = 200p, £0.02 = 2p, £2.22 = 222p, £2.02 = 202p; 2p is the smallest and 222p is the largest.
3–4 **622, 642**
  5 **10** Refer to Paper 7 Q33 on rounding to the nearest pound. 6 is after the decimal, so 9 rounds up to 10.
  6 **9.64** Refer to Paper 16 Q34–37 on dividing by 100. 100p = £1.00 so divide by 100: 964 ÷ 100 = £9.64.
  7 **3440** Refer to Paper 7 Q32 on multiplying by 100. 1 m = 100 cm so multiply by 100: 34.4 × 100 = 3440.
  8 **9** 8 + 7 = 15 and 24 − 15 = 9
  9 **24 km** As the room is square, each of the 4 sides will be the same length: 6 × 4 = 24.
  10 **36 m²** Refer to Paper 5 Q11–12 on area and perimeter: 6 × 6 = 36.
11–16 Refer to Paper 1 Q12–17 on calculating elapsed time.
  11 **30** 09:15 to 09:45 is 30 minutes.
  12 **20** 10:30 to 10:50 is 20 minutes.
  13 **35** 11:25 to 12:00 is 35 minutes.
  14 **45** 09:45 to 10:00 is 15 minutes and 10:00 to 10:30 is 30 minutes: 15 + 30 = 45.
  15 **35** 10:50 to 11:00 is 10 minutes and 11:00 to 11:25 is 25 minutes: 10 + 25 = 35.
  16 **2 hr 45 minutes** 09:15 to 10:00 is 45 minutes; 10:00 to 11:00 is 1 hr; 11:00 to 12:00 is 1 hr; 45 minutes + 1 hr + 1 hr = 2 hrs 45 minutes
17–18 Refer to Paper 15 Q12–14 on rounding.
  17 **300** The 8 in 283 rounds up to 300.
  18 **600** 283 + 283 = 566; the 6 in 566 rounds up to 600.
  19 **150** The 1 in 151 rounds down to 150.
  20 **200** The 5 in 151 rounds up to 200.
21–22 Refer to Paper 1 Q22–29 on negative numbers.
  21 **−3**
  22 **−14 °C, −1 °C, 5 °C**
23–28 Work through the calculations one at a time, making sure to make a note of your answers.
23–24 **11 + 2, 19 − 6**
25–26 **10 − 3$\frac{1}{2}$, 4$\frac{1}{4}$ + 2$\frac{1}{4}$** Use a number line showing halves and quarters to count up and down on. Remember $\frac{2}{4} = \frac{1}{2}$.
27–28 **18 − 13, 5 × 1**
  29 **231** Refer to Paper 1 Q20 on column addition.
30–31 Refer to Paper 2 Q10 on column multiplication.
  30 **5672**   31 **56720**
32–36 Each cup and saucer represents 5 people: at 2pm–3pm 5 × 5 = 25 people had tea, at 3pm–4pm 7 × 5 = 35 people had tea, at 4pm–5pm 13 × 5 = 65 people had tea and at 5pm–6pm 10 × 5 = 50 people had tea.
  32 **60** 25 + 35 = 60
  33 **115** 65 + 50 = 115
  34 **40** 65 − 25 = 40
  35 **£700** Refer to Paper 1 Q20 on column addition and Paper 2 Q10 on column multiplication. 25 + 35 + 65 + 60 = 175; 175 × 4 = 700
  36 **350** 175 had tea altogether on Thursday and 175 × 2 = 350
37–40 This is a number family. The numbers in the equation can be added or subtracted in any order. For example, 32 + 49 = 81 can be inverted to 49 + 32 = 81, 81 − 32 = 49 and 81 − 49 = 32
  37 **49** Invert the numbers.

38 **281** 100 has been added to 32 and to 49. As 100 + 100 = 200 then 200 will be added to the answer.
39 **49** 100 has been added to 32 and to 49. As 100 is being subtracted, the answer will still be 49.
40 **881** 500 has been added to 32 and 300 has been added to 49. As 500 + 300 = 800 then 800 will be added to the answer.

Paper 20 (pages 51–53)

1 **3** 6 + 3 = 9
2 **18** 10 − 8 = 2 so the 4 must have been borrowed from and changed into a 3; 3 − 1 = 2.
3 **35** 3 × 5 = 15 so 1 must have been carried over to the next column: 3 × 3 = 9 and 9 + 1 = 10.
4 **8** Refer to Paper 2 Q26 on short division. Place the decimal in the correct position in the answer space before beginning and complete the calculation as normal. 2.50 ÷ 2 = 1.25. Then refer to Paper 2 Q6–7 on adding decimals and use repeated addition to find how many lots of 1.25 go into 10.00: 1.25 + 1.25 + 1.25 + 1.25 + 1.25 + 1.25 + 1.25 + 1.25 = 10.00
5 **10** 200 ÷ 20 = 10
6 **10:13** Subtract 12 from the minutes: 25 − 12 = 13
7 **20** 2 + 4 + 6 + 8 = 20
8 **30** 85 − 28 = 57; 57 − 27 = 30
9 **57** 27 + 30 = 57
10 **55** 28 + 27 = 55
11–13 Add the numbers shown in each column: Andrea got 20 marks (7 + 4 + 9), Mark got 24 marks (8 + 6 + 10), Deborah got 25 marks (9 + 8 + 8), Stuart got 19 marks (7 + 5 + 7), Alison got 24 marks (8 + 7 + 9) and Steven got 22 marks (9 + 6 + 7).
11 **Deborah**   12 **Stuart**
13 **Stuart** Only Stuart has all marks below 8.
14 **Deborah** Only Deborah has 8 or more for each test.
15 **Mark** Mark got 10 for Test 3.
16 **Andrea** Andrea got 4 for Test 2.
17–18 **Mark, Alison** Mark and Alison both got 24.
19–22 Each smiley face represents 2 children, so count the faces in each row and multiply by 2. Roundabouts = 18, Scenic Railway = 16, Dodgems = 22, Swing-boats = 12 and Go Karts = 8.
19 **10** 22 − 12 = 10
20 **10** 18 − 8 = 10
21 **16**
22 **76** 18 + 16 + 22 + 12 + 8 = 76
23–24 Refer to Paper 2 Q4–5 on subtracting decimals and Paper 2 Q6–7 on adding decimals. Don't forget that 131.5 is the same as 131.50
23 **128.25** 131.50 − 3.25 = 128.25
24 **136.25** 131.50 + 4.75 = 136.25
25–26 **E, C** Use a number line showing halves and quarters. $2\frac{1}{2}$ is the largest amount and 1 is the smallest amount.
27–28 **E, B** $1\frac{1}{4} + 1\frac{1}{4} = 2\frac{2}{4}$; $2\frac{2}{4}$ is the same as $2\frac{1}{2}$.
29 **12** 8 eighths = 1 whole and $\frac{4}{8}$ is the same as $\frac{1}{2}$; $\frac{8}{8} + \frac{4}{8} = \frac{12}{8}$.
30 **$8\frac{1}{2}$** Add all the whole numbers together and then add the fractions; 1 + 1 + 1 + 2 + 2 = 7; $\frac{1}{2} + \frac{1}{2} = 1$ and $\frac{1}{4} + \frac{1}{4} = \frac{1}{2}$; $7 + 1 + \frac{1}{2} = 8\frac{1}{2}$.
31 **10 July** 7 days = 1 week: 3 + 7 = 10.
32 **21st** The first column does not show a date on the Tuesday, so count on from the 7th.
33 **3** Wednesday, Thursday and Friday only show 5 dates.
34 **11 July** A fortnight is 14 days (or 2 weeks); 25 − 14 = 11.
35–40 Refer to Paper 5 Q33–36 on sequences.
35–36 **6, $10\frac{1}{2}$** The sequence is to add $1\frac{1}{2}$: $4\frac{1}{2} + 1\frac{1}{2} = 6$; $9 + 1\frac{1}{2} = 10\frac{1}{2}$.
37–38 **123, 131** The sequence is to add 4: 119 + 4 = 123; 127 + 4 = 131.
39–40 **27, 24** The sequence is to subtract 3: 30 − 3 = 27; 27 − 3 = 24.

Paper 21 (pages 54–55)

1–8 To change analogue time into the 24-hour clock, add 12 to the hours from 1 p.m. to 11 p.m. The 24-hour clock is always written with 4 digits, so the times from 12 a.m. will be written as 00:00, 01:00, 02:00 and so on. The first two digits are the hours and the last two digits are the minutes.
1 **17:00** 5 + 12 = 17, so the time will be 17:00.
2 **23:00** 11 + 12 = 23, so the time will be 23:00.
3 **21:05** 9 + 12 = 21, so the time will be 21:05.
4 **16:22** 4 + 12 = 16, so the time will be 16:22.
5 **14:51** 2 + 12 = 14, so the time will be 14:51.
6 **18:30** 6 + 12 = 18, so the time will be 18.30.
7 **08:45** This is an a.m. time.
8 **10:10** This is an a.m. time.
9 **1** Refer to Paper 2 Q11–20 on place value.
10–13 Refer to Paper 15 Q12–14 on rounding.
10 **240** 3 is rounded up to 4 as it is followed by 6.
11 **500** Refer to Paper 1 Q20 on column addition. 236 + 236 = 472; 4 is rounded up to 5 as it is followed by 7.
12 **60** 5 in the tens place is followed by 5 so it is rounded up to 6.
13 **200 seconds** Refer to Paper 2 Q10 on column multiplication: 4 × 55 = 220; 2 in the hundreds place is followed by 2, so 2 in the tens place is rounded to 0.

14 **400** All the digits are the same, except the 6 in the thousands place which has been decreased by 4. Therefore 400 has been subtracted.
15 **11** 33 and 44 are both answers in the 11 times table, therefore they can both be divided by 11.
16–21 33 and 44 are both multiples of 11, so the heading for the second column must be 11. 44 and 48 are both multiples of 4, so the heading for the third row must be 4. Complete the rest in the same way.

×	10	11	12
2	20	(**22**)	24
3	(**30**)	33	(**36**)
4	(**40**)	44	48
5	50	(**55**)	(**60**)

22–25 There are 100p in £1.00, so multiply the numbers by 100. Refer to Paper 7 Q32 on multiplying by 100.
22 **1474** 14.74 × 100 = 1474
23 **10 030** 100.30 × 100 = 10 030
24 **6002** 60.02 × 100 = 6002
25 **2** 0.02 × 100 = 2
26–28 **36, 54, 72** Use knowledge of the 9 times table.
29–31 **A, C, D** An octagon is a shape with 8 sides.
32 **6** Use knowledge of the 9 times table: 6 × 9 = 54, so only 6 can be bought as 7 will cost £63.
33 **3** 2 trips will only carry 22 children (2 × 11 = 22), so 3 will be needed.
34 **425** Refer to Paper 2 Q9 on using column subtraction. 450 − 25 = 425
35–36 Refer to Paper 1 Q22–29 on negative numbers.
35 **−9 °C**   36 **−31 °C**
37–40 Refer to Paper 10 Q3 on ordering numbers.
37 **1452**   38 **5412**
39 **4682**   40 **8642**

Paper 22 (pages 56–58)

1–7 Refer to Paper 5 Q33–36 on sequences.
1–2 **16, 13** The sequence is to subtract 6, then 5, then 4 and so on; 19 − 3 = 16; 14 − 1 = 13.
3–4 **10, 12** The sequence is to subtract 1 and add 2 alternately; 10 − 1 = 9; 13 − 1 = 12.
5–7 **$11\frac{1}{2}$, $19\frac{1}{2}$, $27\frac{1}{2}$** The sequence is to add 4; $7\frac{1}{2} + 4 = 11\frac{1}{2}$; $15\frac{1}{2} + 4 = 19\frac{1}{2}$; $23\frac{1}{2} + 4 = 27\frac{1}{2}$.
8–13 90° is a right angle, so N to E is 90° and NE to SE is 90°. Clockwise is the same direction the hands move in on a clock and anti-clockwise is the opposite direction.
8 **E**   9 **SE**   10 **N**
11 **NW**   12 **NW**   13 **SE**

14 **5** Refer to Paper 2 Q6–7 on adding decimals and use repeated addition to find the answer: £1.25 + £1.25 + £1.25 + £1.25 + £1.25 = £6.25.
15–16 Refer to Paper 5 Q11–12 on area and perimeter.
15 **280** 2 × 14 = 28, so 20 × 14 = 280
16 **68** 20 + 20 + 14 + 14 = 68
17–24 Refer to Paper 5 Q33–36 on sequences.
17–18 **10, 5** The sequence is to divide by 2; 20 ÷ 2 = 10; 10 ÷ 2 = 5.
19–20 **45, 56** The sequence is to add 11; 34 + 11 = 45; 45 + 11 = 56.
21–22 **120, 140** The sequence is to add 20; 100 + 20 = 120; 120 + 20 = 140.
23–24 **11, 8** The sequence is to subtract 3: 14 − 3 = 11; 11 − 3 = 8.
25–26 The shape is divided into 6 equal sections.
25 **$\frac{1}{6}$** 1 of the 6 sections is dotted.
26 **$\frac{5}{6}$** 5 of the 5 sections are white.
27–28 The shape is divided into 6 equal sections.
27 **$\frac{1}{2}$ or $\frac{3}{6}$**
28 **$\frac{1}{2}$ or $\frac{3}{6}$**
29–30 The shape is divided into 8 equal sections.
29 **$\frac{1}{8}$** 1 of the 8 sections is dotted.
30 **$\frac{7}{8}$** 7 of the 8 sections are white.
31–35

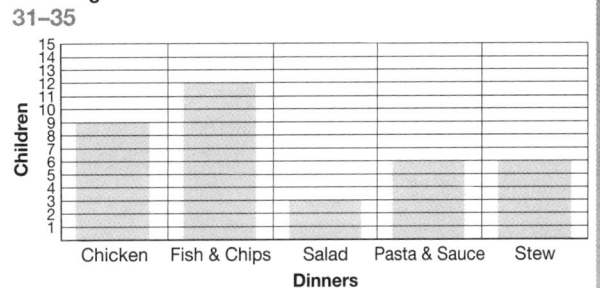

36 **fish and chips** Fish & chips has the highest bar.
37 **salad** Salad has the lowest bar.
39–40 Refer to Paper 2 Q11–20 on place value.
38 **9204**   39 **5075**
40 **140** Refer to Paper 15 Q13–14 on rounding to the nearest 10. 30 is rounded up to 40 as it is followed by 8.

Paper 23 (pages 58–60)

1–3 Refer to Paper 2 Q11–20 on place value.
1 **40**   2 **900**   3 **0**
4–8 Refer to Paper 5 Q33–36 on sequences.
4 **63, 74** The sequence is to add 11: 52 + 11 = 63; 63 + 11 = 74.
5 **17, $19\frac{1}{2}$** The sequence is to add $2\frac{1}{2}$: $14\frac{1}{2} + 2\frac{1}{2} = 17$; $17 + 2\frac{1}{2} = 19\frac{1}{2}$.
6 **11, 7** The sequence is to subtract 4: 15 − 4 = 11; 11 − 4 = 7.

EXPANDED ANSWERS

7–8 **13, 21** The sequence is to add consecutive pairs of numbers to make the next: 5 + 8 = 13; 8 + 13 = 21.

9–15 Multiply the amounts by 2 in the 'Half price' column to complete the 'Ordinary price column'. Divide the amounts in the 'Ordinary price' column by 2 to find the missing amounts in the 'Half price' column. Refer to Paper 2 Q31 on multiplying decimal numbers. Place the decimal in the correct position in the answer before beginning and complete the calculation as normal.

9 **£4.90** 9.80 ÷ 2 = 4.90
10 **£2.60** 5.20 ÷ 2 = 2.60
11 **£5.80** 2.90 × 2 = 5.80
12 **£3.70** 7.40 ÷ 2 = 3.70
13 **£5.20** 2.60 × 2 = 5.20
14 **£5.10** 10.20 ÷ 2 = 5.10
15 **£9.40** 4.70 × 2 = 9.40

16–20 Refer to Paper 2 Q26 on short division and divide all the numbers by 3. Only the numbers that do not have a remainder are exactly divisible by 3.

16–18 **69, 405, 3**
19–20 **237, 852**
21–32 Refer to the key words on page 1.
33 **cube** An edge is the straight line where 2 faces meet on a 3D shape. The only 3D shapes shown are a cube and a tetrahedron. A tetrahedron has 6 edges and a cube has 12.
34 **100** Refer to Paper 15 Q12–14 on rounding. The 50 in 50 rounds up to 100.
35–40 **3521, 3512, 2531, 2513, 1532, 1523** Refer to Paper 10 Q3 on ordering numbers.

Paper 24 (pages 60–62)

1 **57** 33 + 24 = 57
2 **74** 38 + 11 + 25 = 74
3–4 **Beechton, 47** Going through Beechton is 14 + 33, which is 47 km; going through Sheldon is 38 + 16, which is 54 km; Beechton is the shorter journey.
5–6 **Applegate, 49** Going through Applegate is 33 + 16, which is 49 km; going through Maryland is 14 + 38, which is 52 km; Applegate is the shorter journey.
7–14 Refer to Paper 19 Q37–40 on number families.
7 **248** 100 has been added to 27 and 21. As 100 + 100 = 200 then 200 will be added to the answer.
8 **27** Invert the numbers shown in the calculation: 48 − 21 = 27.
9 **748** 500 has been added to 27 and 200 has been added to 21. As 500 + 200 = 700 then 700 will be added to the answer.

10 **227** Invert the numbers in the calculation so 27 is the answer: 48 − 21 = 27; 200 has been added to 48, therefore 200 will be added to the answer.
11 **368** 200 has been added to 52 and 100 has been added to 16. As 200 + 100 = 300 then 300 will be added to the answer.
12 **968** 800 has been added to 52 and 100 has been added to 16. As 800 + 100 = 900 then 900 will be added to the answer.
13 **52** Invert the numbers shown in the calculation: 68 − 16 = 58.
14 **552** 700 has been added to 68 and 200 has been added to 16. As 700 − 200 = 500 then 500 will be added to the answer.
15 **pentagon** A shape with 5 sides is called a pentagon.
16 **0** There are no shapes that have 4 sides the same length.
17 **heptagon** A shape with 7 sides is also sometimes referred to as a septagon.
18–25 Refer to Paper 5 Q33–36 on sequences.
18–19 **$8\frac{1}{2}$, 10** The sequence is to add $1\frac{1}{2}$: $7 + 1\frac{1}{2} = 8\frac{1}{2}$; $8\frac{1}{2} + 1\frac{1}{2} = 10$.
20–21 **36, 45** The sequence is to add 3: 33 + 3 = 36; 42 + 3 = 45.
22–23 **42, 22** The sequence is to subtract 4: 42 − 4 = 38; 26 − 4 = 22.
24–25 **5p, 11p** The sequence is to add 3p: 2p + 3p = 5p; 8p + 3p = 11p.
26–34 Refer to Paper 12 Q15–26 on completing a timetable and Paper 1 Q12–17 on calculating elapsed time.

	Begins	Ends
First lesson	09:40	10:10
Second lesson	10:10	10:40
Break	10:40	11:00
Third lesson	11:00	11:30
Fourth lesson	11:30	12:00

35–39 There are 1000 ml in 1 litre. Refer to Paper 1 Q20 on column addition, Paper 2 Q26 on short division and Paper 2 Q9 on using column subtraction.
35 **4** Use repeated addition to find the answer: 250 + 250 + 250 + 250 = 1000 ml.
36 **B** Divide 1000 ml by 2 to find half of 1 litre: 1000 ÷ 2 = 500.
37 **C** 1000 − 750 = 250
38 **250** 1000 − 750 = 250
39 **3** Use repeated addition to find the answer: 250 + 250 + 250 = 750.
40 **3276** Refer to Paper 2 Q10 on column multiplication.

Paper 12

1. It is now 2:37 p.m. In half an hour's time it will be ____ : ____ p.m.
2. What time is a quarter of an hour before midnight? ____ : ____ p.m.
3. Six minutes after 10:45 is ____ : ____

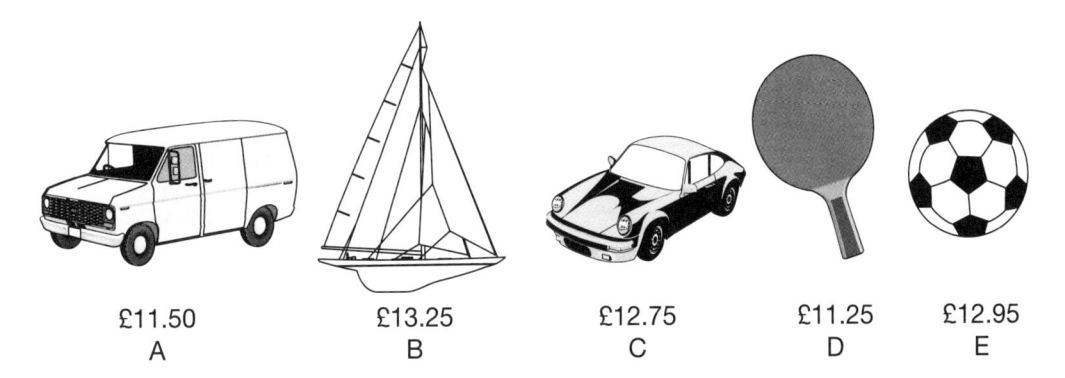

£11.50 A £13.25 B £12.75 C £11.25 D £12.95 E

4–5. Which two toys could you buy with £23.00? ____ and ____

6. How much would it cost to buy the bat and the football? £ ____

7. How much change would you have from £13.00 if you bought a van (A)? £ ____

8. How much change would you have from £15.00 if you bought a boat (B)? £ ____

9. How much would it cost to buy all the toys? £ ____

10. How much would it cost to buy a van and two bats? £ ____

11–14. Draw the lines of **symmetry** in each of the following shapes. The first one has been done for you.

15–26 The table below should show the important times in the morning at Greenway Primary School.

Each lesson is half an hour long. Break lasts 15 minutes. Lessons begin at 09:30.

Fill in the correct times.

	Begins	**Ends**
First lesson		
Second lesson		
Break		
Third lesson		
Fourth lesson		
Fifth lesson		

27–30 Join each three-dimensional object on the left with its **net** on the right by drawing a line.

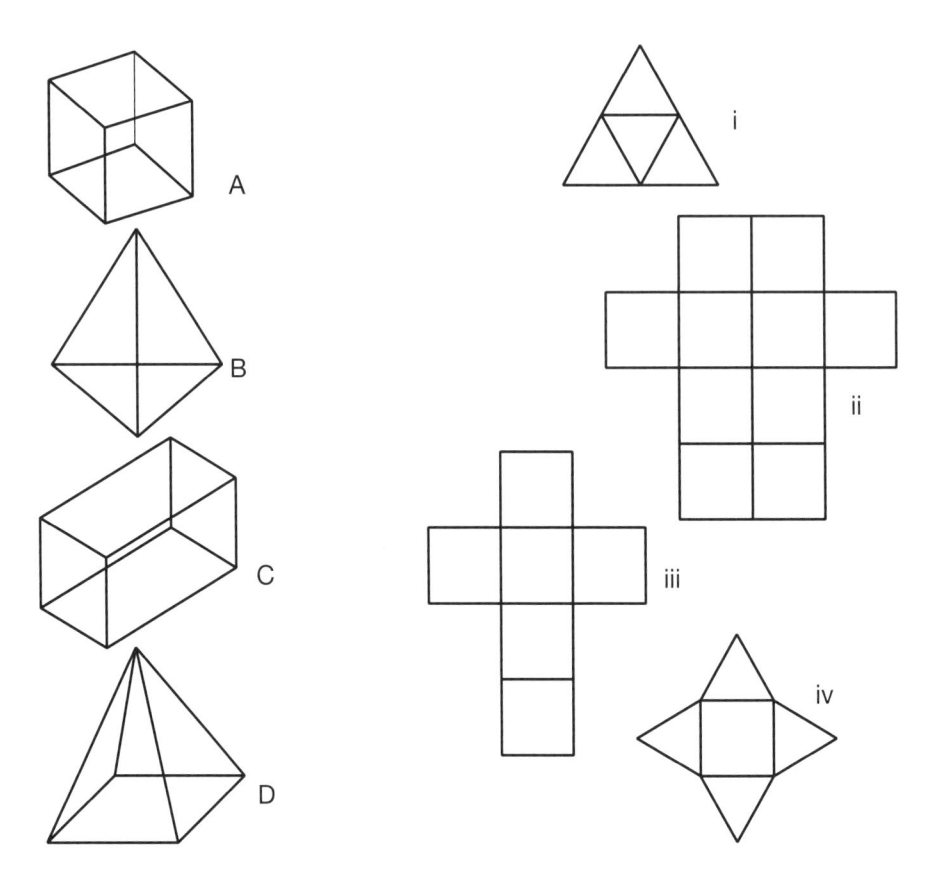

31 What is the difference between 1 litre and 850 ml? _____ ml

The children in a swimming club made this **pictogram**.

It shows how many children of each age group could swim.

Age 7	♀♀
Age 8	♀♀♀♀
Age 9	♀♀♀♀♀♀♀♂
Age 10	♀♀♀♀♀♀♀♀♀
Age 11	♀♀♀♀♀♀♀♂

Key

♀ = 2 children

♂ = 1 child

32 How many children in the club can swim? _____

33 How many more 10-year-olds than 8-year-olds can swim? _____

Swimming group A has all the 10-year-olds and 11-year-olds.

Swimming group B has all the younger children.

34 Which is the larger group? _____

35 How many more are in this group? _____

A season ticket for the swimming baths costs £15.00 each.

36 If all the children bought a season ticket, what would be the total cost? _____

Last Thursday there was a 100 m race. Two of the 9-year-olds entered along with all the 10- and 11-year-olds.

37 How many were in the race? _____

38 The rest of the children entered the 50 m race. How many were in this race? _____

39 What is the remainder when 28 is divided by 5? _____

40 What is the remainder when 28 is divided by 6? _____

Now go to the Progress Chart to record your score!   Total   40

Paper 13

Use two of the numbers in the brackets to complete the following **sums**. Do not use the same combination twice.

1–2 _____ + _____ + 9 = 12   (1, 2, 3, 4, 5, 6, 7, 8)

3–4 _____ + _____ + 8 = 12   (1, 2, 3, 4, 5, 6, 7)

5–6 _____ + _____ + 7 = 12   (1, 2, 3, 4, 5, 6)

7–8 _____ + _____ + 7 = 12   (1, 2, 3, 4, 5, 6)

9–10 _____ + _____ + 6 = 12   (1, 2, 3, 4, 5)

11–12 _____ + _____ + 6 = 12   (1, 2, 3, 4, 5)

13–14 _____ + _____ + 5 = 12   (1, 2, 3, 4)

15–18 Use the numbers in the brackets below only once to make each side of the square add up to 12. You can use the **sums** above to help you.

(1, 2, 3, 5)

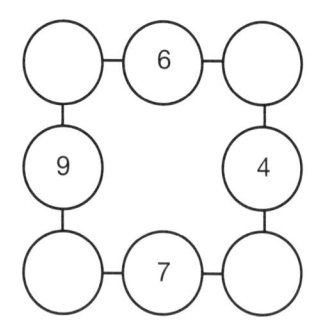

19–23 Make these shapes look the same on each side of the **mirror line**.

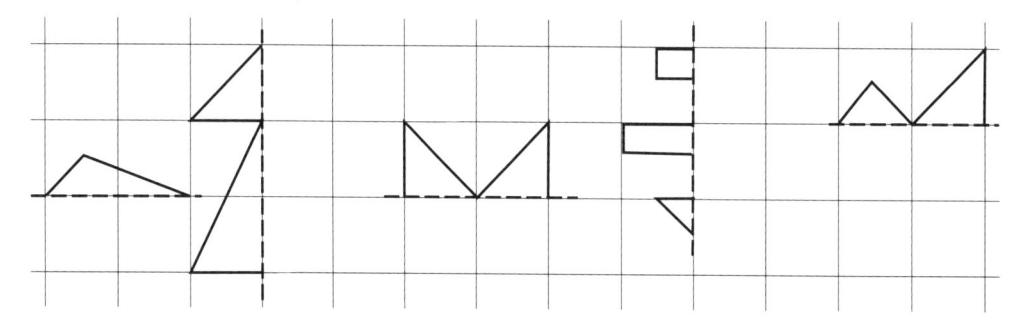

Put a sign in each space so that each question will be correct.

24 6 _____ 6 = 4 _____ 3

25 4 _____ 5 = 3 _____ 3

26 6 _____ 2 = 3 _____ 1

27 7 _____ 4 = 4 _____ 1

28 8 _____ 2 = 5 _____ 1

29 7 _____ 1 = 4 _____ 4

This bar chart shows how many people got on a bus at each of the four stops in the centre of the town.

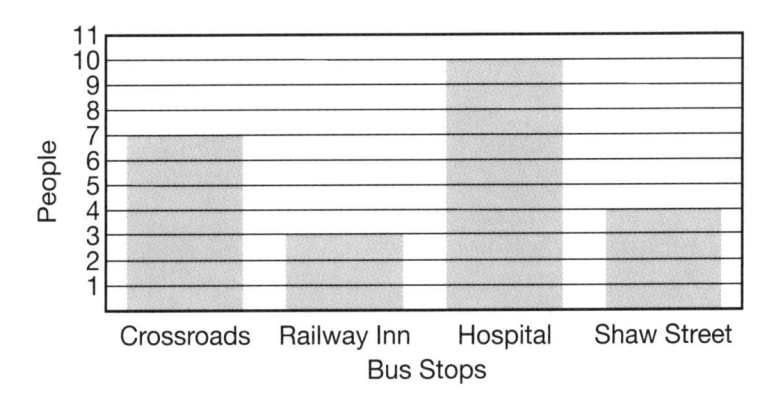

30 How many people got on the bus altogether? _____

31 How many more people got on at the hospital than at the Railway Inn? _____

32 How many more people got on at the crossroads than at Shaw Street? _____

33 How many more people got on at Shaw Street than at the Railway Inn? _____

34 If all the people who got on the bus paid 60p each, how much was this altogether? £ _____

A quarter of the passengers got off the bus at the next stop and 3 more got on.

35 Now how many passengers would be on the bus? _____

Mrs Andrews 18 kg

Mr Bell 8.6 kg

Mrs Clark 17.1 kg

Mr Dring 21.4 kg

Mr Eliot 14.8 kg

Passengers cannot take more than 16 kg on the plane.

36–37 Who was allowed to take all their luggage with them?

_____ and _____

38 Whose luggage is the heaviest? _____

39 How much over 16 kg is his case? _____

40 How much extra weight would Mr Bell be allowed to put in his case to make it up to 16 kg? _____

Now go to the Progress Chart to record your score!   Total   40

Paper 14

Write the next two numbers in each line.

1–2	115	110	105	100	___	___
3–4	27	31	35	39	___	___
5–6	543	538	533	528	___	___
7–8	213	219	225	231	___	___
9–10	66	77	88	99	___	___

11 How many times can I take 7 from 98? _____

Underline the correct answer in each line.

12 12 × 11   = 112   121   123   132   144

13 400 ÷ 20 = 40   20   200   400   4

14 101 − 89 = 12   11   21   23   22

15 $\frac{1}{2}$ hour   = 15 min 20 min 30 min 40 min 45 min

16 70 × 40 = 280   2800   1100   240   470

17 603 ÷ 3 = 21   31   301   201   210

18 My watch is 9 minutes slow. It shows 5 minutes to 11. What is the right time? ___ : ___

19 When a number is taken away from 21 the answer is 8. What is the number? _____

36

20
```
   27
   68
   49
+  36
─────
```

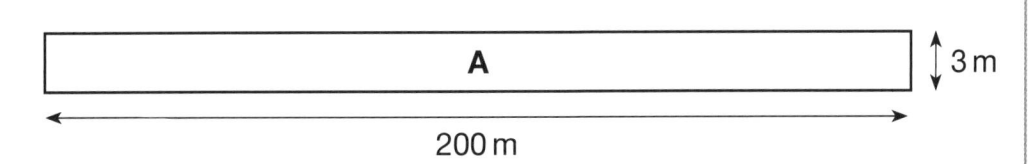

21
```
   403
×   70
─────
```

A — 200 m × 3 m

22 What is the **area** of rectangle A? _____ m²

23 What is the **perimeter** of rectangle A? _____ m

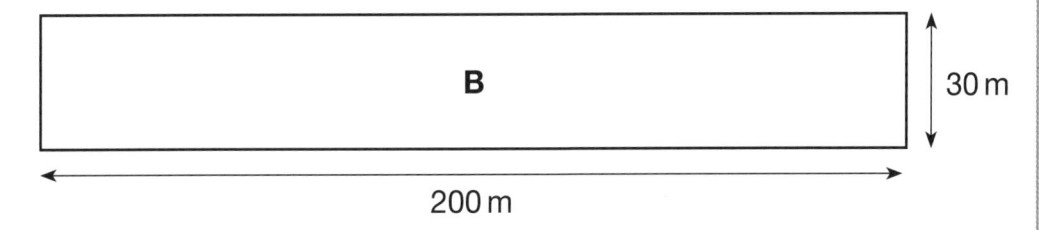

B — 200 m × 30 m

24 What is the **area** of rectangle B? _____ m²

25 What is the **perimeter** of rectangle B? _____ m

26 How many times bigger is the **area** of rectangle B than the **area** of rectangle A?

27 By how much is the **perimeter** of B bigger than the **perimeter** of A?

28 From the **digits** 7, 8 and 9 make a number so that 9 is the hundred and 8 is the unit.

29 What is the **product** of 10 and 100?

Write the answers to the following questions.

30 $12 \times 8 = 10 \times 8 + 2 \times 8 =$ _____

31 $15 \times 7 = 10 \times 7 + 5 \times 7 =$ _____

32 $18 \times 5 = 10 \times 5 + 8 \times 5 =$ _____

33 $16 \times 9 = 10 \times 9 + 6 \times 9 =$ _____

My brother has 40 counters.

18 are yellow, 15 are green and the rest are blue.

34 How many are blue?

35 How many times can I take 6 from 72?

To make a rosette you need 15 cm of ribbon.

36 How many could you make with a metre of ribbon?

37 How much ribbon would be left over?

38 What is the **sum** of the odd numbers smaller than 10?

39 What needs to be added to change 5864 to 7864?

40 What needs to be subtracted to change 6842 to 6342?

Now go to the Progress Chart to record your score! Total 40

Paper 15

1–2 Fill in the missing numbers on this number line.

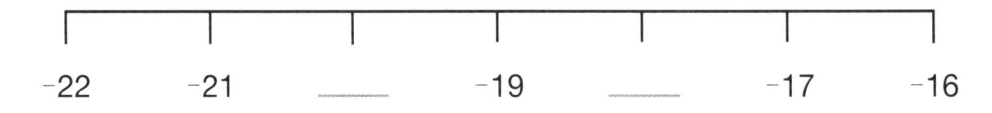

−22   −21   ____   −19   ____   −17   −16

3 How many weeks are there in 28 days?

Here is part of a centimetre ruler.

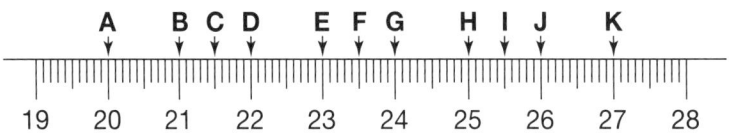

4 How far is it from A to B?

5 How far is it from D to G?

6 How far is it from G to K?

7 How far is it from F to H? _____

8 What is the distance between A and C? _____

9 How far is it from A to K? _____

10 How far is it from B to J? _____

11 What is the distance from C to F? _____

12 The film lasted 153 min, which is _____ min to the nearest 100 min.

13 Oxton to Cowster is 197 miles, which is _____ miles to the nearest 10 miles.

14 The return trip (from Oxton to Cowster and back) is _____ miles to the nearest 10 miles.

    A   B   C   D   E

15–17 Shade in the **quadrilaterals**.

18 What is the **product** of 6 and 21? _____

You start with 16 eggs. Half are broken so you throw them away. Half of the unbroken eggs are too old so you throw them away.

19 You are now left with _____ good eggs.

20 Twice nine is _____

21 How many children are in the class? _____

22 How many children are wearing grey socks? _____

23 How many are wearing black shoes? _____

24 _____ children are wearing grey socks and black shoes.

25 How many children are not wearing black shoes? _____

26 _____ are not wearing grey socks.

27 I spend 27p. What change should I receive if I give the shopkeeper £1.00? _____ p

The time is 5 to 8. How fast or slow are these clocks?

Write the number of minutes and ring the correct word for each clock

28–29 _____ minutes   fast   slow

30–31 _____ minutes   fast   slow

32–33 _____ minutes   fast   slow

34–35 _____ minutes   fast   slow

36 What needs to be added/subtracted to change 7812 to 7212? _____

37 What needs to be added/subtracted to change 6324 to 6354? _____

38 What is the largest number you can make with these **digits**: 2, 5, 8, 6, 5? _____

39 Now write it in words.
_____

40 Write in figures four thousand, one hundred and twenty. _____

Now go to the Progress Chart to record your score!   Total   40

Paper 16

1–3 What fraction of the board is shaded? Underline the correct answers.

$\frac{1}{2}$ $\frac{1}{3}$ $\frac{1}{6}$ $\frac{1}{12}$ $\frac{2}{3}$ $\frac{2}{6}$ $\frac{2}{12}$ $\frac{3}{6}$ $\frac{3}{12}$ $\frac{6}{12}$

4–5 What fraction of the paperclips has been ringed? Underline all the correct answers.

$\frac{1}{2}$ $\frac{1}{3}$ $\frac{1}{4}$ $\frac{1}{6}$ $\frac{2}{3}$ $\frac{2}{4}$ $\frac{2}{6}$ $\frac{3}{4}$ $\frac{3}{6}$

6 Which fraction is larger: $\frac{1}{2}$ or $\frac{1}{4}$? _____

Put a circle round the correct answer.

7 0.25 = $\frac{1}{2}$ $\frac{2}{5}$ $\frac{1}{4}$ $\frac{25}{10}$

8 0.1 = $\frac{1}{2}$ $\frac{1}{1}$ $\frac{1}{10}$ $\frac{1}{100}$

9 In a sponsored swim, Kevin's dad says he will pay 50p per length.

Kevin swims 13 lengths, so his dad has to pay   £ _____

10 Which town is furthest away from Nottingham? _____

11 Which town is nearest to Nottingham? _____

12 Brighton is further away from Nottingham than Southampton is by _____

13 Cardiff is further away from Nottingham than Leeds is by _____

14 What is the distance from Nottingham to Southampton to the nearest 10 km? _____ km

15 What is the distance from Nottingham to Leeds to the nearest 10 km? _____ km

16 Write in figures: eight thousand and eighteen. _____

17–19 Carefully draw the hands on the clocks on the right so they show the same times as those on the left.

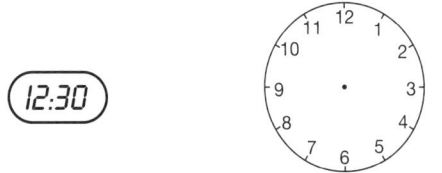

12:30

Remember that the hour hand is shorter than the minute hand.

02:45

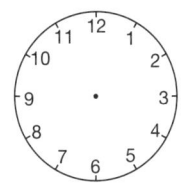

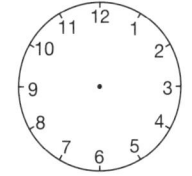

01:30

20 $\frac{1}{2}$ of 26 = _____

21 $\frac{2}{3}$ of 21 = _____

22 $\frac{3}{4}$ of 16 = _____

23 6 paper chains at 80p cost £_____ .

24 6 strands of tinsel at 85p cost £_____ .

25 How many Christmas cards, at 45p can I buy with £2.00? _____

Alison weighs 39 kg, Christopher weighs 37.5 kg and Rachel weighs 41.7 kg.

26 Alison and Christopher together weigh _____ kg

27 How much heavier is Alison than Christopher? _____ kg

28 Christopher and Rachel together weigh _____ kg

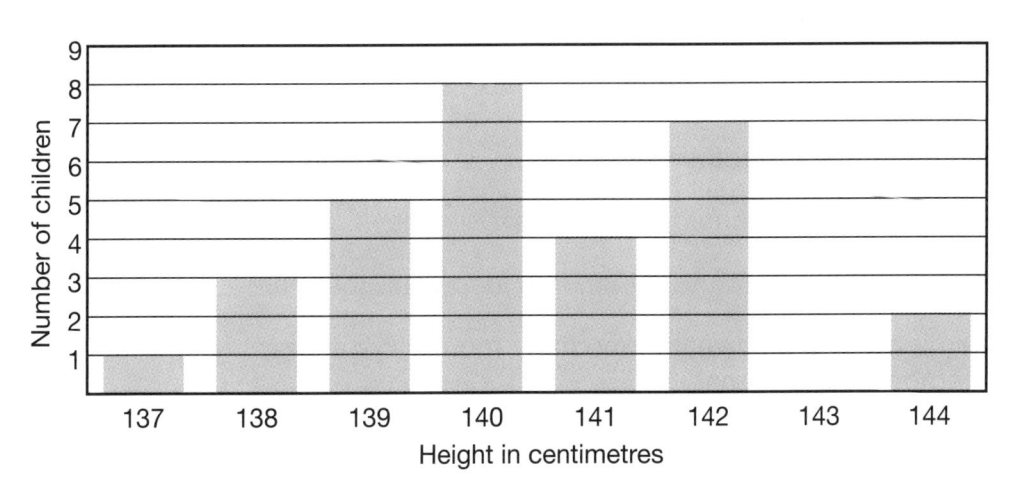

29 How many children are shown on the bar chart? _____

30 How many children are 143 cm tall? _____

31 How many more children are 140 cm tall than are 138 cm? _____

32 How many children are less than 140 cm tall? _____

33 How many children are more than 140 cm tall? _____

34 4 m 25 cm + 5 m 75 cm = _____ m

35 8 m 36 cm + 7 m 68 cm = _____ m

36 5 m 0 cm − 2 m 45 cm = _____ m

37 6 m 10 cm − 2 m 70 cm = _____ m

38–39 If 5 m of material costs £6.00, 1 m will cost _____ and 11 m will cost _____.

40 How many $\frac{1}{2}$ hour lessons are there between 09:30 and 12:00? _____

Now go to the Progress Chart to record your score!   Total 40

Paper 17

Thirty days has September,
April, June and November.
All the rest have 31,
Except February alone
Which has but 28 days clear,
And 29 in each leap year.

1 In June and July together there are _____ days.

2 In March and April together there are _____ days.

3 In February and March together, in a leap year, there are _____ days.

4 When it is not a leap year, how many more days are in December than February? _____

5 How many years are there in 48 months? _____

6 How many years in a millennium? _____

7   What fraction of the picture above is dotted? _____

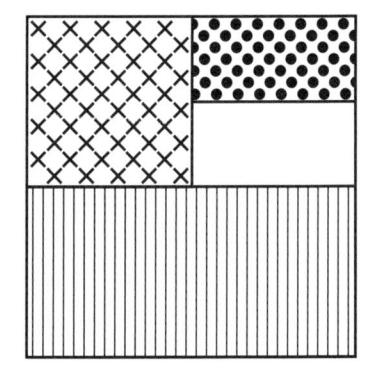

8   What fraction is striped? _____

9   What fraction is plain? _____

10 What fraction has crosses? _____

11 If three pencils cost 99p what will be the cost of two pencils? _____ p

12 What is the **product** of 7 and 6? _____

13 If 12 books cost £66.00 what is the cost of one book? _____

Put a sign in each space so that each question will be correct.

14–15   7 __ 1 = 4 __ 4

16–17   3 __ 7 = 5 __ 2

18–19   6 __ 1 = 8 __ 1

20–21   6 __ 4 = 2 __ 12

22–23   4 __ 4 = 10 __ 6

24–25   12 __ 3 = 8 __ 2

26–27   2 __ 7 = 15 __ 1

28–29   3 __ 1 = 7 __ 4

30   428
      × 7
      ____

31   3.29
      × 6
      ____

32   3.24
      × 7
      ____

This diagram shows that one whole can be divided into thirds, sixths and twelfths.

1 Whole												
$\frac{1}{3}$				$\frac{1}{3}$				$\frac{1}{3}$			
$\frac{1}{6}$		$\frac{1}{6}$		$\frac{1}{6}$		$\frac{1}{6}$		$\frac{1}{6}$		$\frac{1}{6}$	
$\frac{1}{12}$	$\frac{1}{12}$	$\frac{1}{12}$	$\frac{1}{12}$	$\frac{1}{12}$	$\frac{1}{12}$	$\frac{1}{12}$	$\frac{1}{12}$	$\frac{1}{12}$	$\frac{1}{12}$	$\frac{1}{12}$	$\frac{1}{12}$

33 How many $\frac{1}{3}$s make 1?

34 How many $\frac{1}{12}$s make $\frac{2}{3}$?

35 How many $\frac{1}{6}$s make $\frac{1}{3}$?

36 How many $\frac{1}{12}$s make 1?

37 How many $\frac{1}{6}$s make $\frac{2}{3}$?

38 How many $\frac{1}{6}$s make 1?

39 How many $\frac{1}{12}$s make $\frac{5}{6}$?

40 How many $\frac{1}{3}$s make $\frac{8}{12}$?

Now go to the Progress Chart to record your score!   Total   40

Paper 18

Write the next two numbers in each of the following lines.

1–2	£1.75	£1.50	£1.25	£1.00	___	___
3–4	30p	36p	42p	48p	___	___
5–6	2015	2025	2035	2045	___	___
7–8	$\frac{1}{2}$	1	$1\frac{1}{2}$	2	___	___
9–10	1 day	20 hr	16 hr	12 hr	___	___
11–12	132	140	148	156	___	___

13 22.5
   +18.6
   ─────

14 26.5
   + 36.5
   ─────

15 38.9
   + 43.8
   ─────

Fill in the missing numbers in each of these questions.

16 4 × _____ = 12

17 2 + 3 + _____ = 11

18 5 × 6 = _____

19 12 − _____ = 8

20 24 + _____ = 30

21 How many years in 60 months?

Eve bought a book for £4.75 and some writing paper for £1.80.

22 How much did she spend? £_____

23 How much change would she have from £10.00? £_____

24 The school hall has 32 rows of chairs and there are 20 chairs in each row. How many chairs are there altogether?

25 What is the **product** of 7 and 12?

26–29   × 4 →

14	
21	
16	
23	

30–34   ÷ 6 →

54	
36	
42	
150	
186	

35 How many erasers for 5p each could you buy with £6.85?

36 50 × 1 = 60 − _____

37 20 × 0 = 7 − _____

47

Put the hands on these clocks.

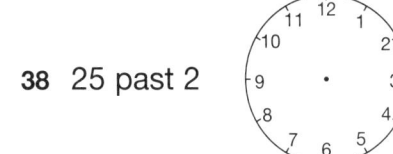

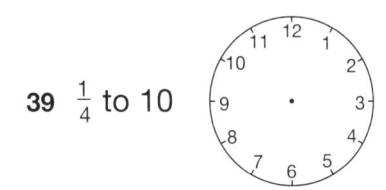

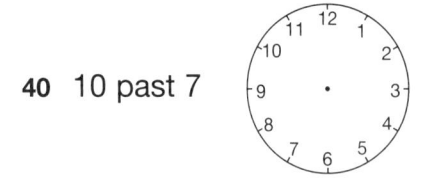

38 25 past 2

39 $\frac{1}{4}$ to 10

40 10 past 7

Now go to the Progress Chart to record your score! Total 40

Paper 19

1–2 Underline the smallest and circle the largest.

22p,   £2,   £0.02,   £2.22,   £2.02   202p

3–4 Underline the smallest and circle the largest.

623   632   642   640   622   624

5 **Round** to the nearest pound: £9.66 = £ _____

6 Write 964p in £.   964p = £ _____

7 Write metres in centimetres: 34.4 m = _____ cm

8 The age of Bridget, Bob and Sarah add up to 24 years.

If Bob is 8 and Bridget is 7, how old is Sarah?

One side of a **square** room is 6 m.

9 How far is it all round?

10 What is the **area** of the **square** floor?

Here is a timetable for Wednesday morning.

Mathematics	09:15–09:45
Music	09:45–10:30
Break	10:30–10:50
History	10:50–11:25
Games	11:25–12:00

11 We do mathematics for ____ min.

12 Break is ____ min long.

13 We play games for ____ min.

14 We spend ____ min having our music lesson.

15 How long is the history lesson? ____ min.

16 From 09:15 to 12:00 is ____ hour ____ min.

17 London to Leeds is 283 miles, which is ____ miles to the nearest 100 miles.

18 The return trip (to Leeds and back) is ____ miles to the nearest 100 miles.

19–20 The fuel tank in a truck holds 151 litres, which is ____ litres to the nearest 10 litres and ____ litres to the nearest 100 litres.

21 Fill in the missing number in the brackets on this number line.

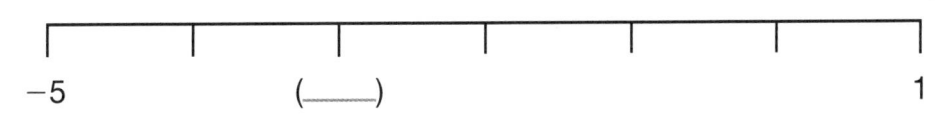

−5   (____)   1

22 Put these temperatures in order, lowest first.

5 °C   −14 °C   −1 °C   ____ ____ ____

Underline the two questions in each line which give the answer.

23–24 $13 =$ $9 + 3$ 7×2 $11 + 2$ $19 - 6$ $14 + 1$

25–26 $6\frac{1}{2} =$ $12\frac{1}{2} - 6\frac{1}{2}$ $10 - 3\frac{1}{2}$ $4 + 2$ $5\frac{1}{4} + 2\frac{1}{4}$ $4\frac{1}{4} + 2\frac{1}{4}$

27–28 $5 =$ $10 - 10$ 20×5 $18 - 13$ $15 - 5$ 5×1

29	88 77 + 66	**30**	709 × 8	**31**	709 × 80

Here is a **pictogram** which shows the number of people who had tea at Meg's Café last Thursday.

🍵 represents 5 people having tea.

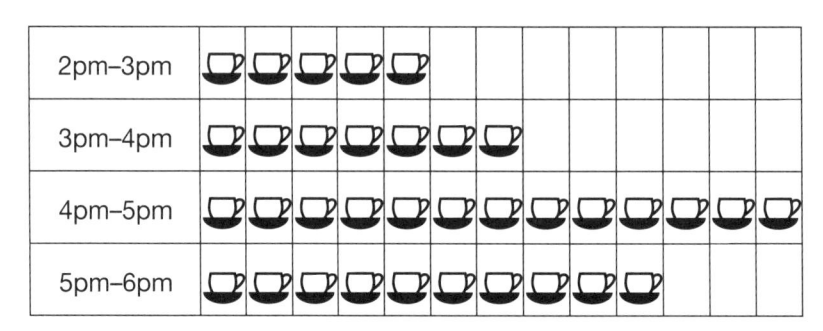

2pm–3pm	🍵🍵🍵🍵🍵
3pm–4pm	🍵🍵🍵🍵🍵🍵🍵
4pm–5pm	🍵🍵🍵🍵🍵🍵🍵🍵🍵🍵🍵🍵🍵
5pm–6pm	🍵🍵🍵🍵🍵🍵🍵🍵🍵🍵

32 How many people had tea at Meg's Café between 2 p.m. and 4 p.m.? _____

33 How many had tea between 4 p.m. and 6 p.m.? _____

34 How many more people had tea between 4 p.m. and 5 p.m., than between 2 p.m. and 3 p.m.? _____

35 If the café charged £4 for a tea how much money was taken last Thursday? _____

Twice the number of people who had tea at Meg's Café on Thursday had tea there on Saturday.

36 How many were there on Saturday? _____

Look at this **sum** carefully.

$$32 + 49 = 81$$

Now use it to help you with the following questions.

37 81 – 32 = _____ **38** 132 + 149 = _____

39 181 – 132 = _____ **40** 532 + 349 = _____

Paper 20

Fill in the missing numbers so that each question will be correct.

1. 2_
    + 46

    69

2. 40
    − __

    22

3. __
    × 3

    105

4. Rakesh gets £2.50 pocket money a week.

   If he saves half of it, how long will it take him to save £10.00? _____ weeks

5. How many times can I take 20 from 200? _____

6. A clock is 12 minutes fast. What is the correct time when the clock shows 10:25? ___ : ___

7. Find the **sum** of all the even numbers between 1 and 9. _____

8. There are 85 children in Classes 1, 2 and 3. If there are 28 in Class 1, and 27 in Class 2, how many are there in Class 3? _____

9. How many are there in Classes 2 and 3 together? _____

10. How many are there in Classes 1 and 2 together? _____

Here are the marks some children got in the last three spelling tests (out of 10).

	Andrea	Mark	Deborah	Stuart	Alison	Steven
Test 1	7	8	9	7	8	9
Test 2	4	6	8	5	7	6
Test 3	9	10	8	7	9	7
Totals						

11. Who had the highest total marks? _____

12. Who had the lowest total marks? _____

13. Who got fewer than 8 marks in each of the tests? _____

14 Who got 8 or more marks in each of the tests? _____

15 Who got 10 in one test? _____

16 Who had fewer than 5 marks in one test? _____

17–18 _____ and _____ got the same total marks.

Look at the **pictogram** and answer the questions.

Roundabouts	☺☺☺☺☺☺☺☺☺
Scenic Railway	☺☺☺☺☺☺☺☺
Dodgems	☺☺☺☺☺☺☺☺☺☺
Swing-boats	☺☺☺☺☺☺
Go Karts	☺☺☺☺

Key
☺ represents 2 people

19 How many more children went on the dodgems than on the swing-boats? _____

20 There were ____ fewer children on the go karts than on the roundabouts.

21 How many children went on the scenic railway? _____

22 What was the total number of children who went on these amusements? _____

Maria is 131.5 cm tall. Susan is 3.25 cm shorter than Maria.
Cathy is 4.75 cm taller than Maria.

23 How tall is Susan? _____ cm

24 How tall is Cathy? _____ cm

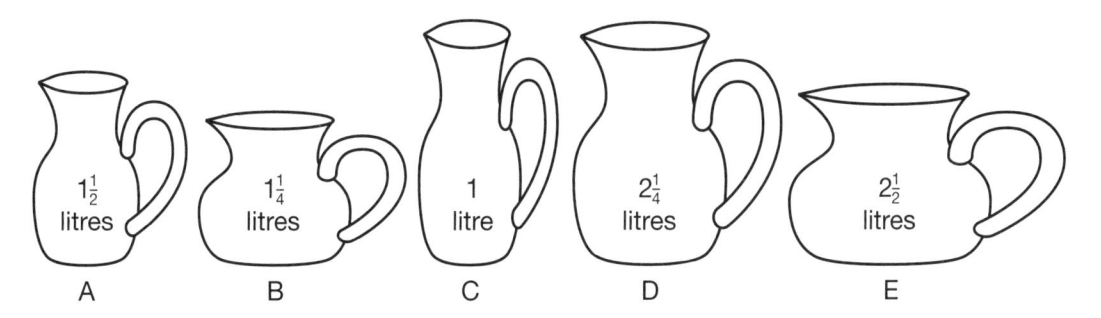

Jugs: A $1\frac{1}{2}$ litres, B $1\frac{1}{4}$ litres, C 1 litre, D $2\frac{1}{4}$ litres, E $2\frac{1}{2}$ litres

25–26 Jug _____ holds the most and jug _____ holds the least.

27–28 Jug _____ holds exactly twice as much as jug _____.

29 A beaker holds $\frac{1}{8}$ litre. How many beakers full of water can be poured from jug A? _____

30 What is the total amount that all the jugs will hold? _____

July					
Sunday		5	12	19	26
Monday		6	13	20	27
Tuesday		7	14	21	28
Wednesday	1	8	15	22	29
Thursday	2	9	16	23	30
Friday	3	10	17	24	31
Saturday	4	11	18	25	

31 If today's date is July 3rd, what will be the date in one week's time? _____

32 What is the date on the third Tuesday in July? _____

33 How many days appear 5 times in this July? _____

34 A fortnight before July 25th is _____

Fill in the missing numbers in each line.

35–36 $1\frac{1}{2}$ 3 $4\frac{1}{2}$ _____ $7\frac{1}{2}$ 9   _____   12

37–38 115   119   _____   127   _____   135   139

39–40 36   33   30   _____   _____   21   18

Now go to the Progress Chart to record your score!   Total ⬜ 40

Paper 21

Write these times for the 24-hour clock.

1. 5 p.m. ____:____
2. 11 p.m. ____:____
3. 9:05 p.m. ____:____
4. 4:22 p.m. ____:____
5. 2:51 p.m. ____:____
6. 6:30 p.m. ____:____
7. 8:45 a.m. ____:____
8. 10:10 a.m. ____:____

9. What number needs to go in the box?

    2341 = 2000 + 300 + 40 + ☐

10. A ladder is 236 cm long, which is ____ cm to the nearest 10 cm.

11. Two ladders are ____ cm to the nearest 100 cm.

12. A chocolate biscuit lasts Amy 55 seconds, which is ____ seconds to the nearest 10 seconds.

13. How long will it take her to eat 4 at the same speed, to the nearest 100 seconds? ____

14. What needs to be added/subtracted to change 8621 to 8221? ____

15. What number will divide 33 and 44? ____

16–21 Here is part of a tables chart. Complete the empty brackets.

×			
	20	( )	24
	( )	33	( )
	( )	44	48
	50	( )	( )

22. How many pence in £14.74? ____
23. How many pence in £100.30? ____
24. How many pence in £60.02? ____
25. How many pence in £0.02? ____

26–28 Which of these numbers are exactly **divisible** by 9? Underline them.

15   24   36   46   54   62   72   84   95   98   107

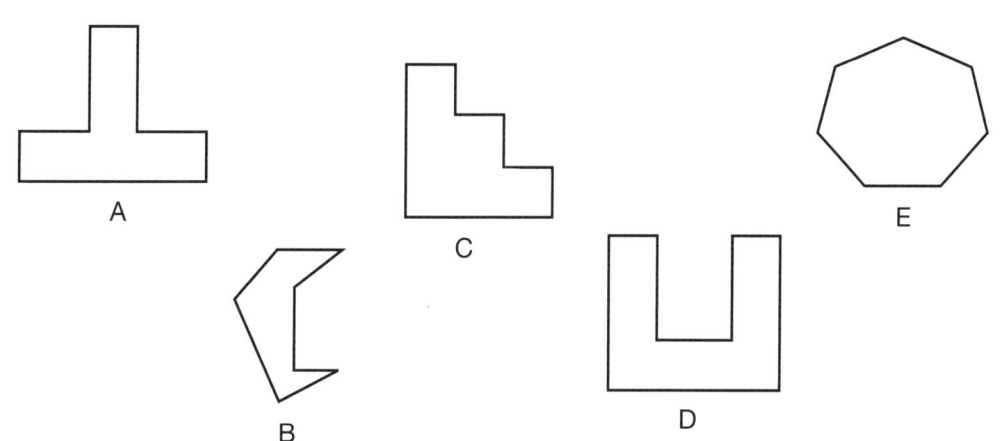

29–31 Colour in any **octagons** below.

A   C   E

B   D

32 Tickets for a concert cost £9.
How many tickets can I buy with £60? _____

Twenty-five children are going to a swimming pool by a minibus which can take 11 passengers.

33 How many trips must the minibus make? _____

34 Write the correct number in the box.

450   →   25 less is   [   ]

35 Draw a circle around the lowest temperature: −7 °C   −9 °C
36 Draw a circle around the lowest temperature: −31 °C   −30 °C

Put a ring round the smallest and underline the largest in each line.

37–38   5412   1452   4251   2415   2514   5214
39–40   8426   4862   6824   8642   6842   4682

Now go to the Progress Chart to record your score!   Total   40

Paper 22

Fill in the missing numbers in each line.

1–2 34   28   23   19   ___   14   ___

3–4 ___   9   11   10   12   11   13   ___

5–7 $3\frac{1}{2}$ $7\frac{1}{2}$ ___ $15\frac{1}{2}$ ___ $23\frac{1}{2}$ ___

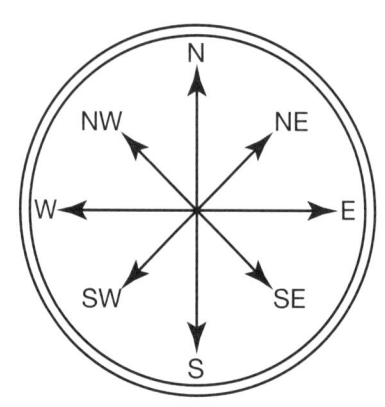

Can you name these compass points?

8 90° clockwise from N is ___

9 90° anticlockwise from SW is ___

10 2 right-angles clockwise from S is ___

11 3 right-angles anticlockwise from SW is ___

12 2 right-angles anticlockwise from SE is ___

13 2 right-angles clockwise from NW is ___

14 If a goldfish costs £1.25, how many can I buy for £6.25? ___

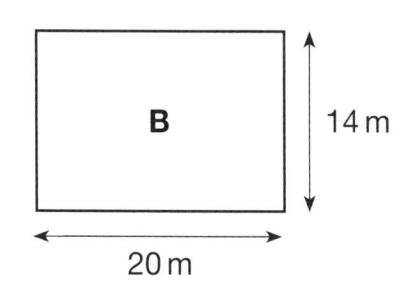

15 What is the **area** of rectangle B? ___ m²

16 What is the **perimeter** of rectangle B? ___ m

Complete the following lines.

17–18 80   40   20   ____   ____

19–20 12   23   34   ____   ____

21–22 60   80   100   ____   ____

23–24 20   17   14   ____   ____

Write the correct fraction in its lowest form in each space.

25 Dotted ____

26 White   ____

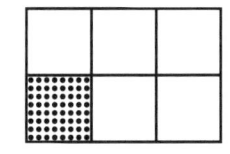

27 Dotted ____

28 White   ____

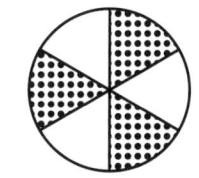

29 Dotted ____

30 White   ____

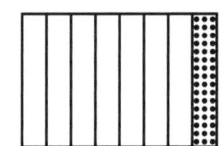

31–35 A class of 36 children voted for their favourite school dinners and then made a chart.

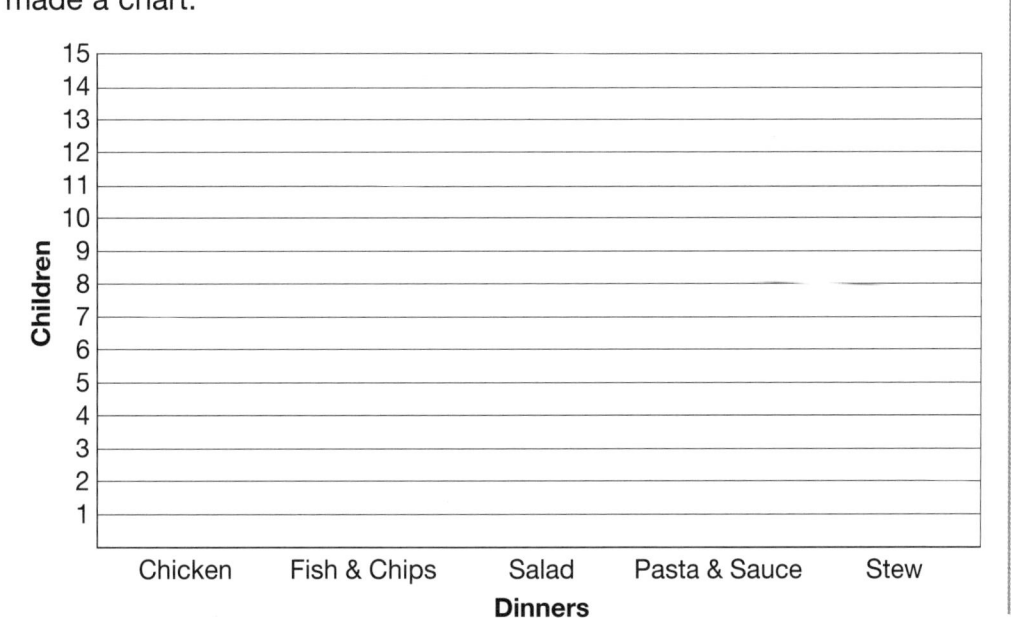

Children (y-axis: 1 to 15)

Dinners (x-axis): Chicken, Fish & Chips, Salad, Pasta & Sauce, Stew

Shade in the columns to show how they voted:

- 3 children voted for salad.
- 3 times as many voted for chicken.
- One third of the class voted for fish and chips.
- The number who voted for stew was one half of the number who voted for fish and chips.
- Both sets of twins in the class, plus two other children, voted for pasta and sauce.

36 The most popular school dinner was _____

37 The least popular school dinner was _____

38 Write in figures nine thousand, two hundred and four. _____

39 Write in figures five thousand and seventy-five. _____

40 The TV programme lasted 138 minutes, which is _____ min to the nearest 10 min.

Now go to the Progress Chart to record your score!   Total   40

Paper 23

What number needs to go in the box?

1 5842 = 5000 + 800 + ☐ + 2

2 1906 = 1000 + ☐ + 0 + 6

3 2340 = 2000 + 300 + 40 + ☐

Write the next two numbers in these lines.

4	8	19	30	41	52	___	___
5	$4\frac{1}{2}$	7	$9\frac{1}{2}$	12	$14\frac{1}{2}$	___	___
6	31	27	23	19	15	___	___
7–8	1	2	3	5	8	___	___

9–15 Complete the following sales board.

SALE	
Ordinary price	Half price
£9.80	
£5.20	
	£2.90
£7.40	
	£2.60
£10.20	
	£4.70

Underline the numbers which are divisible by 3.

16–18	69	101	58	405	521	3
19–20	602	73	237	35	852	484

Write the name **semicircle, equilateral triangle, isosceles triangle, quadrilateral, pentagon, hexagon, heptagon, cube, tetrahedron** or **parallelogram** under the correct shapes.

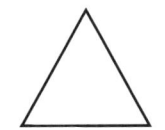

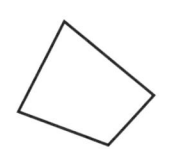

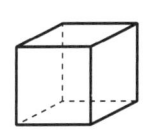

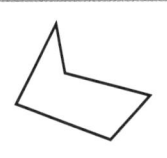

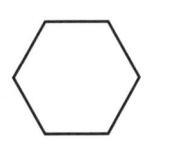

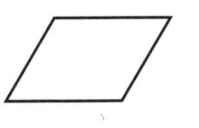

21

22

23

24

25

26

27

28

29

30

31

32

33 Which of the shapes on the page before has the most edges? _____

34 James weighs 50 kg, which is _____ kg to the nearest 100 kg.

35–40 Put these numbers in order, largest to smallest.

3512   2531   3521   1523   2513   1532

_____   _____   _____   _____   _____   _____

Now go to the Progress Chart to record your score!   Total   40

Paper 24

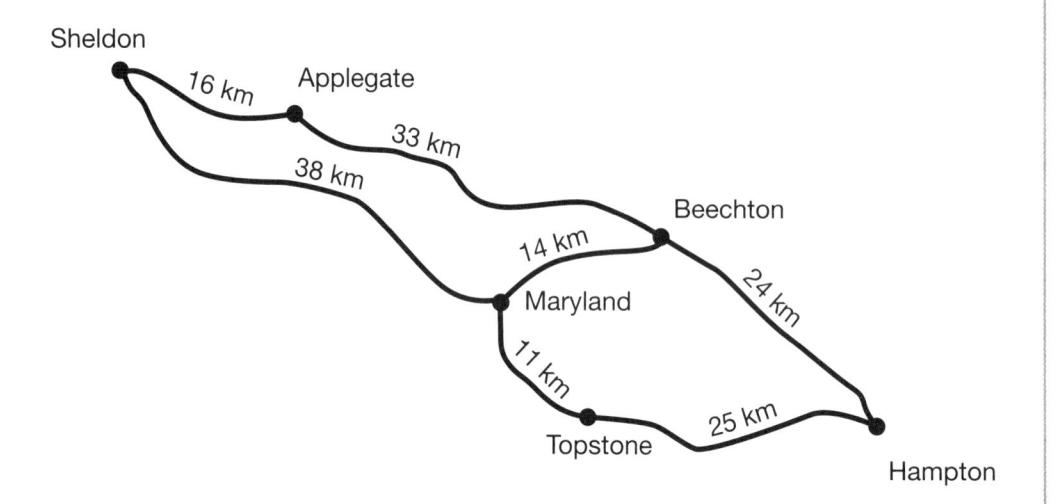

1 From Applegate to Hampton (going through Beechton) is _____ km.

2 From Sheldon to Hampton (going through Maryland and Topstone) is _____ km.

3–4 The shortest journey from Maryland to Applegate goes through _____ and is _____ km long.

5–6 The shortest journey from Beechton to Sheldon goes through _____ and is _____ km long.

60

Look at this calculation carefully and use it to help you with the following questions.

    27 + 21 = 48

7 127 + 121 = ____

8 48 − 21 = ____

9 527 + 221 = ____

10 248 − 21 = ____

Here is another example and set of questions.

    52 + 16 = 68

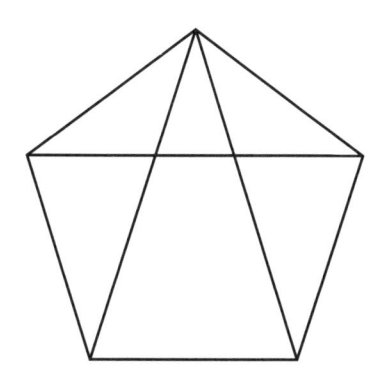

11 252 + 116 = ____

12 852 + 116 = ____

13 68 − 16 = ____

14 768 − 216 = ____

15 What is the name of the outside **polygon**?

16 How many **squares** can you find in the polygon?

17 What is the name of a polygon with seven sides?

Fill in the missing numbers in each line.

18–19 $2\frac{1}{2}$ 4 $5\frac{1}{2}$ 7   ____   ____

20–21 33   ____   39   42   ____   48

22–23 ____   38   34   30   26   ____

24–25 2p   ____   8p   ____   14p   17p

Southcross School has 4 half-hour lessons each morning.

26–34 The lessons start at 9:40 and there is a break of 20 minutes after the 2nd lesson. Fill in the timetable.

	Begins	**Ends**
First lesson	09:40	
Second lesson		
Break		
Third lesson		
Fourth lesson		

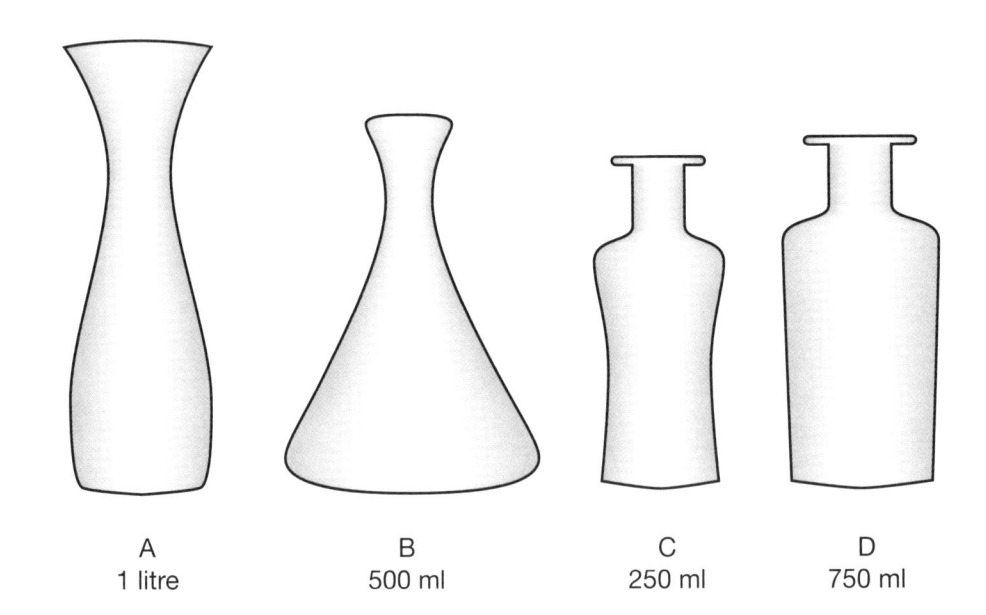

A
1 litre

B
500 ml

C
250 ml

D
750 ml

35 How many times could you fill bottle C from bottle A? ____

36 Bottle A holds twice as much as bottle ____ .

37 Bottle D and bottle ____ together hold as much as A.

38 How much more does A hold than D? ____ ml

39 How many times could you fill C from D? ____

40 468 × 7 = ____

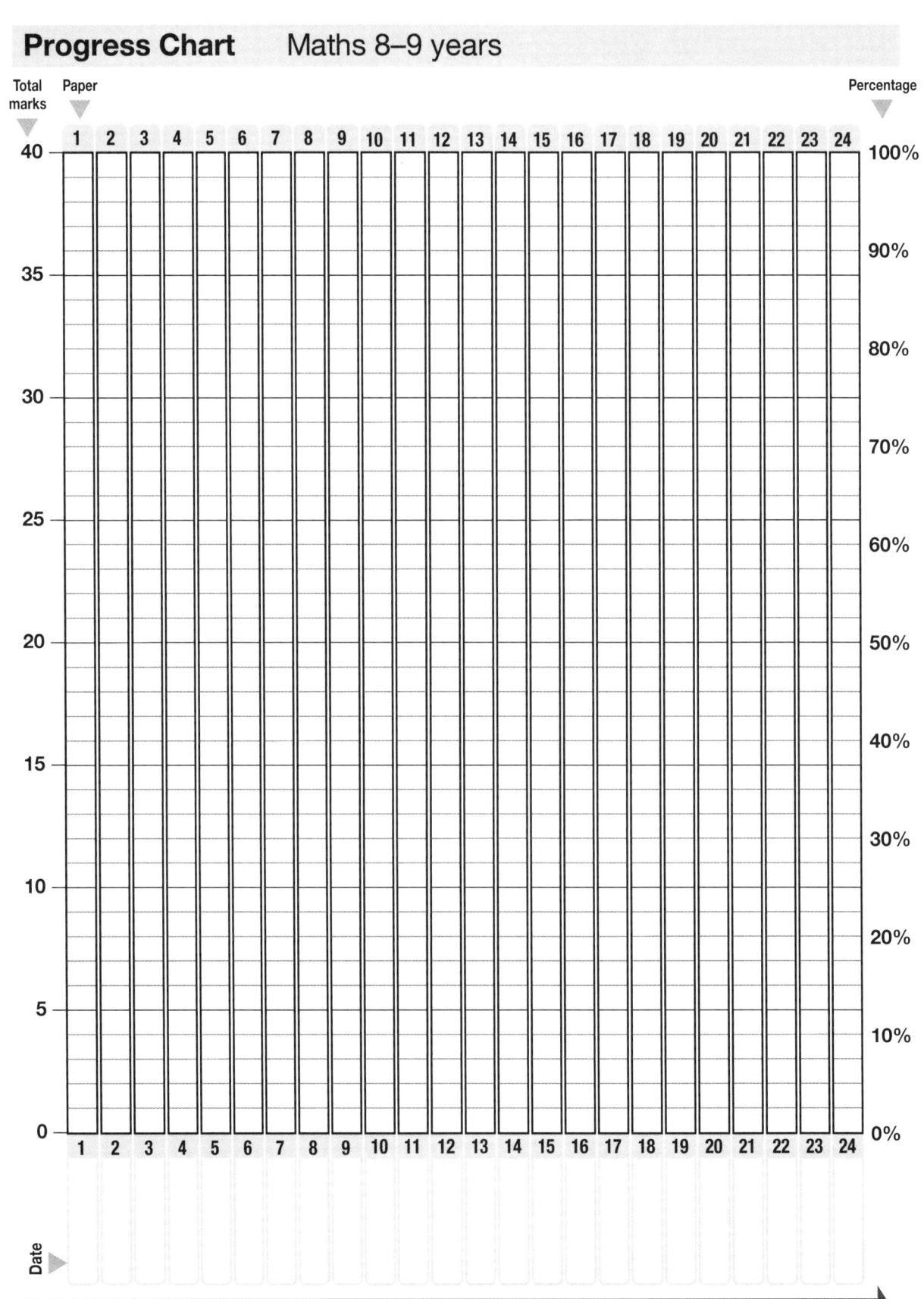

Progress Chart   Maths 8–9 years

Total marks

Paper: 1 2 3 4 5 6 7 8 9 10 11 12 13 14 15 16 17 18 19 20 21 22 23 24

Percentage: 0%, 10%, 20%, 30%, 40%, 50%, 60%, 70%, 80%, 90%, 100%

Date

When you've finished the book read the Next Steps